The Nature of Consciousness, the Universe and Everything

An Inquiry into emergent consciousness
from microbes to humans and beyond

ALEX MILOV

ISBN: 0-9992294-0-0
ISBN-13: 978-0-9992294-0-8

ACKNOWLEDGEMENT

When I set out on this project, I was not sure where it would lead. Describing the nature of consciousness, the universe and everything is, after all, a pretty tall order. I am very happy to report the book has turned out to be much more than I hoped for. It only now becomes clear to me that I didn't write the book at all. The book wrote itself. I am not using poetic license. Instead, I am sharing a profound truth you too will see as you awaken to the nature of consciousness, the universe and everything.

CONTENTS

RATIONALE

The Labyrinth of Greek mythology was an elaborate maze designed and built for King Minos of Crete. It held the dreaded Minotaur, a half man and half beast which devoured the sacrificial Athenian youth offered as retribution for the death of the King's son.

The labyrinth was so cunningly constructed no one could find their way to defeat the Minotaur. Ultimately, the king's daughter gave Theseus a golden thread which enabled him to enter, slay the Minotaur and find his way out again thereby saving the Athenian youth from their terrible fate.

People of ancient Greece found meaning and purpose in a rich tradition of storytelling we call mythology. This is how they learned about the nature of the universe and what it meant to be Greek. Every culture has a way of transmitting its beliefs about the nature of the universe and what it's like to be part of that culture. The sum of these understandings is the culture's Worldview.

Worldview is like a map of the universe. Everyone's worldview is unique. Take any two cultures or any two individuals, dig deep enough and you will find divergence. Furthermore, all worldviews change over time. So not only can we be assured any two cultures or any two individuals will have divergence, any single culture or individual will in time conflict with itself. Understanding the dynamics of worldviews is important because those with similar worldviews tend to get along well while those with differing worldviews tend to interact contentiously.

Historically, changes in worldview unfolded more gradually. During the last century, through the media new voices gained influence shifting the culture with dramatic changes such as the civil rights movement, the anti-war movement, the women's rights movement and anti-apartheid. The most influential voices in the public square were journalists, academic activists, politicians, and clergy. Their influence hinged on public perceptions of their honesty, accuracy, and integrity. Things have changed.

The bandwidth has widened, and the playing field leveled. A multitude of special interest groups ranging from environmental support groups to climate change deniers now clamors for attention. Each of these micro-cultures has an agenda with sometimes violently conflicting worldviews. Sadly, in the struggle for airtime, the primary qualification is no longer honesty, accuracy or integrity. Instead, it is the most exciting and sensational messages which tend to capture attention.

The anger, fear, and lust of heated controversy are more attractive than reasoned discussion. Honesty as a cultural value has become so degraded, and misrepresentations have become so familiar, we have become desensitized to the propaganda. Our ability to recognize misinformation and to meaningfully weigh the evidence has eroded. The outcome is increased polarization with distorted worldviews. We have lost our way.

Everyone believes their own worldview is "right." Many see the worldviews of others as ignorant, maladjusted or even evil. "They" are the problem. If "they" would change, all would be well in the world. Well-intended efforts on both sides seem only to make matters worse.

How are we to make sense of it all? With the cacophony of contentious contradictory claims of "truth" bantered about, one sometimes feels lost in a modern labyrinth at risk of being devoured by a Minotaur of half-truths, misunderstandings, and deliberate distortions. How then shall we find our way? Well, that is exactly what this book is about; its primary purpose is to raise our consciousness and broaden our worldviews. It is by awakening to the nature of consciousness itself that we will be provided with a golden thread to lead us out of the labyrinth.

PREFACE

This book is an inquiry into the nature of consciousness. When consciousness is properly understood, healthy life choices become apparent. To understand consciousness, we need to understand several related subjects. The journey is challenging but very much worthwhile. The information compiled here allows for nothing less than an awakening as to who we are in the universe. Though the evidence comes from naturalistic observations and the methods are based on the principles of science, the destination is ultimately spiritual.

I didn't know it at the time, but I began writing this book as a psychology professor at a small private college years before sitting down to compose it. I enjoyed teaching. I wanted my classes to be both useful and fun. Teaching the same subjects day and night over several years, I began to see connections between psychological constructs. What today seems obvious to me wasn't even on my radar screen back when I began teaching. I think I can help others see.

Occasionally we come upon a map while at the mall or the zoo designed to help us find our way. As we try to understand our situation, the arrow next to the words "you are here" orients us. Knowing our position and the lay of the land helps us see the steps necessary to get where we want to go. Psychotherapy is a lot like the "you are here" experience. If you listen carefully, many casual conversations are also like the "you are here" experience. The social world helps us stay oriented.

Successful navigation usually requires valid information. An accurate map, drawn to scale is invaluable. In addition to location, it is helpful to know where we have been and where we want to go, and we should understand the properties of the vehicle in which we travel (ourselves). Payload, fuel economy, road handling characteristics, service requirements all these play into likely outcomes. People who consider these things carefully tend to succeed and flourish.

So this book hopes to come to terms with some pretty big questions. What is the nature of the universe, who am I, what is our purpose, and how do we get where we need to go. As I look back at the map of my own life, it seems the universe has had an almost magical way of revealing itself. I sometimes find connections which appear to be more than simple coincidence, and one of these occurs to me now.

In my youth I read a book that captured my imagination, "The Hitchhiker's Guide to the Galaxy," by Douglas Adams. It has something of a cult following. I remember being comforted when I began grad school as I noticed a reference to the book on the wall of my mentor's office. I was safe; he understood.

Now, many years later, I am in a state of mental goose flesh as I realize I have taken on the audacious task of trying to answer that book's laughable central question: "The Meaning of Life, the Universe, and Everything." So I have entitled my book, "The Nature of Consciousness, the Universe, and Everything," is in honor of the joy and insight offered by Douglas Adams. As I begin the project I am surprised and delighted to realize I just happen to be living on Adams Street.

1 COMPARE AND CONTRAST

Understanding is a dynamic, transitional, and relational process. Facts, on the other hand, are usually thought of as static and unchanging. Most people prefer facts over understanding. We find comfort in ideas which seem to be written in stone. It just feels good to have a sense of certainty in an uncertain world. This is why some people recoil from the idea that all facts are contingent upon other facts for their factuality. Information without context is nonsense because understanding is a dynamic, transitional, and relational process.

I remember a little game I played as a child repeating a word over and over again until the word seemed to lose all meaning. For example, if you repeat the word "hamburger" often enough in rapid succession, it begins to take on the same absence of meaning as the nonsense word "zabart." Psychologists call this semantic satiation. It happens as the clusters of neurons responsible for processing the context of the word habituate to the repetition. When these neurons temporarily fail to respond in the usual way, the word loses meaning. Context is essential to understanding because understanding is a dynamic, translational and relational process.

To say something is a dynamic, transitional and relational is to draw attention to the conditions surrounding its occurrence. The word dynamic begins the description because first and foremost, understanding is never static. It is always "in motion." This movement is said to be transitional to contrast it with the simple back and forth oscillation between states. Understanding must have an expansive quality for it to have meaning, it must lead somewhere. And lastly, understanding is relational because the associations of understanding are not random. Instead, they are usually based on the rules of logic. When facts are associated in a dynamic, transitional and relational way they induce the type of consciousness we call understanding.

Though I didn't realize it at the time, my understanding of understanding began with a conversation I had with my mentor back in grad school. We were walking across the campus as he assigned me a task. I remember feeling a little proud as we made our way through the corridor when I grasped the full meaning of the assignment. I said with a measure of confidence and satisfaction, "Oh, you mean, compare and contrast." He paused, and with a slightly pained look on his face he said, "Well that is all there is." He made it sound like everybody knew this. At the time it hurt my feelings, but I have since come to appreciate what Dr. James Rotten shared with me that day.

In essence, we understand something precisely to the extent we are able to compare and contrast that thing with everything else. In other words, understanding emerges by placing objects and ideas into appropriate categories of association while excluding them from inappropriate categories. Understanding just is the compare and contrast process of grouping ideas based on content and context.

The children's television show Sesame Street uses a learning song about comparing with the lyrics, "One of these things is not like the other, one of these things doesn't belong." At this point in the song lesson, the child inspects the four items being displayed for inspection. Three are somehow alike and the fourth is somehow categorically different. This is compare and contrast learning in pure form.

Okay, for you skeptics out there who take issue with the idea that understanding is simply a matter of comparing and contrasting concepts under consideration, you may be thinking "Where is your evidence, prove it." I like your style; however, we must be careful with our demands. Strictly speaking, science or any other human endeavor can not prove anything. The best we can do is tally the evidence and make what are essentially probability statements about the likely nature of reality.

The only thing we can say with certainty is the evidence seems to suggest a given proposition is true. It is important to keep in mind new information may come along invalidating conclusions previously taken to be true. We need to have an open mind if we hope to see things accurately. All that said, there is some good evidence supporting the idea understanding emerges from compare and contrast categorization. In fact, here we have a rather high degree of confidence because the evidence has what researchers call convergent validity.

When the same finding is seen using completely independent ways of measuring, our confidence in the result increases. Researchers call this kind combined evidence "convergent validity." The thinking goes like this: the odds are small any two separate independent measuring instruments will both be wrong in the same way. Since more than one avenue of independent investigation supports the idea under consideration, we have greater confidence the convergent evidence accurately reflects reality.

The first bit of evidence I will offer suggesting knowing emerges from compare and contrast categorizations comes from logically grinding out the idea that we understand something based on how we relate that thing to everything else. It just makes sense compare and contrast is how we come to understand the universe.

Take, for instance, the concept or category called

"eyeglasses." One way to understand eyeglasses is to categorize them as objects usually worn on the face which correct vision. That is, eyeglasses fall into the category of things used for vision correction. A more thorough understanding includes the idea eyeglasses are similar to but different from sunglasses. So the broader category "glasses" includes things which can correct the focus of an image and things which can reduce the intensity of light striking the retina. Then there is a category called "prescription sunglasses" which bridges these two categories. And so it goes. All of these items fall into the broadest category "glasses," but a more refined understanding comes with additional categories of understanding each with different properties. The more accurately we categorize items based on the similarities and differences in their properties, the more complete is our understanding. And so we have logically developed evidence supporting the idea knowing emerges from compare and contrast categorization. Convergent evidence for this comes from many examples of independent research including research on academic performance.

Because understanding emerges from compare and contrast categorization, it makes sense that more categories equals more understanding. As such, we would expect children with more categories of understanding to have greater academic success (more demonstrated knowledge) than children with fewer categories of understanding. Research on academic achievement often finds vocabulary to be one of the strongest predictors of educational success (e.g. Lee, 2011). Children who understand more words perform better than children who know fewer words. Since words are the abstract representations of objects and categories, more words equal more knowledge.

As vocabulary increases, the number of available

categories increases. As the number of categories increase, knowledge increases. As knowledge increases, educational success increases. Most people tend to guess socioeconomic status to be the strongest predictor of academic achievement. Though socioeconomic status also predicts success, vocabulary is a better predictor. If you want your kids to do well in school, teach them plenty of words!

So we have now developed convergent evidence supporting the idea that "knowing" is based on the compare and contrast process of categorization. To review, convergent validity method of support number one, logically grinding out the idea knowing is based on compare and contrast. The second method of support, independent research suggesting vocabulary predicts academic performance. Taken together we now have increased confidence understanding emerges from the compare and contrast process of categorization. The universe makes sense.

I will do my best to categorize the ideas presented in this book correctly. If an idea is contentious, I hope to demonstrate why it belongs in the category assigned. Proper categorization is not as easy as it sounds. Some concepts initially appear to belong in one category, but upon further consideration are found to belong in a different category. All categories are perfectly good, but problems do arise when we make mistakes, especially when we claim to have more knowledge than we actually have.

To illustrate this point, let me share a little story. As a young parent, I decided it was important to be completely honest with my daughter. Having been something of a troubled youth myself, I wanted to minimize her difficulties, and it seemed rigorous honesty was the best way to achieve the goal. She has since graduated from a prestigious law school, passed the bar on the first try and is happily married to her high school sweetheart. I am very proud of them both, and I think the honesty helped.

When she was about six, the honesty policy was put to a test. She had heard rumors in school that Santa Claus wasn't real. She asked me directly. What could I say to an innocent six-year-old little girl about Santa Claus while still being honest? Perhaps a historical perspective, "many years ago there was a man..." No, that didn't feel right. Maybe I could say, "I'm Santa Claus." No, not what this pivotal moment in child rearing demanded. When dealing with the belief system of a six-year-old, nothing but the deepest most self-searching honesty will do. So I told my daughter the whole truth. I said, "I don't know!"

I can imagine a collective rumbling response from the readers, "Oh, brother, now the guy has come completely unhinged, doesn't even know there is no such thing as Santa Claus." Allow me to continue. I went on to tell her that I didn't see how one person could go to everyone's house in one night. I then conceded that, though I had my doubts, it was possible there was a Santa Claus and perhaps he had abilities beyond my current understanding. In telling her the truth, I simply offered her my knowledge of the evidence and allowed her to draw her own conclusions. As the sage advised, "Do not seek truth; seek only the release of cherished opinion." For the record, I am pretty sure there is no Santa Claus.

Consciousness is the unfolding process of comparing and contrasting for the purpose of increasing survival. The most basic category of compare and contrast awareness is probably the continuum of pain and pleasure. Pain and pleasure are nature's way of motivating behavior. For healthy organisms, these motivated behaviors tend to increase survival.

Neonates are primarily reflexive at birth. In just a few short years, a consciousness emerges able to use language and logic to categorize complex ideas and experiences. Most four-year-olds can perform the categorization task with ease. Think again about the Sesame Street song lyrics "One of these things is not like the other" this time sung while displaying a drinking glass, a teacup, a coffee mug, and a bowl. The lyrics are "One of these things is not like the others; one of these things doesn't belong. Can you guess which thing is not like the others before I finish my song?" Well, can you guess?

Of course, the answer is a glass because the other objects are non-transparent, or a bowl because the others are for drinking out of, or a coffee mug because the others rarely have writing or logos printed on them or a teacup because the others rarely use saucers. As you can see, this little game gets complicated fast. Context is essential, and it is easy to be led astray.

Children enjoy fairy tales in part because they are easy to follow. The context has been well-established. As soon as they hear the words "once upon a time," they know they can sit back, relax and enjoy the ride. Things might get a little dicey, but everything is under control, it is all in good fun, and it will all turn out alright in the end. Upon hearing the words "and they all lived happily ever after," they understand the story is over. Life once again makes sense, time for bed.

Understanding is always a relational process. It is like a fabric of intertwined threads of context and inter-related categories of understanding. For example, the word "red" has meaning when considered within a context. Most of us learned about colors a long time ago, so we quickly find a way to comprehend the word "red." That is, color is the context most people use when they hear the word "red."

Years ago I had a neighbor who was also called "Red." It takes a little extra cognitive processing to shift gears and consider ideas outside of their familiar context. For this reason, when exploring new areas, it often feels like we are starting in the middle. It is sometimes a little hard to get a toe hold because there is no effective, "once upon a time" or color chart to orient us.

I remember feeling this way when I took chemistry. Much of what I was learning was outside of my experience. I had little context for the new information. It was hard to find an anchor point for the new data. It was as if I had to juggle the relationships in the air while at the same time looking around for the right place to put them down. I kept dropping pieces until a sufficient critical mass of information was set in place. Once the context was established, everything seemed to snap into place, and it all suddenly made sense.

If I were to draw a large circle on the board of an astronomy classroom, you might think I was trying to depict a planet or a star. This assumption is context exerting its influence. If I were to add two radius lines, thereby sectioning out a small wedge, you would probably see I was making a pie chart. Imagine a pie chart with a thin slice shaded red. This small wedge represents everything we think we know. Now imagine a second slice adjacent to the first also quite small, shaded green. This slice represents everything we believe we do not know. The vast majority of the chart apart from these two thin slices represents the information we don't know we don't know. This perspective is not an exercise in humility. It is the most accurate and useful mindset we can bring to any inquiry.

Art, science, religion, and philosophy all provide valuable insight. Each informs within its own context, and I have received benefit from each I doubt could have found in the others. However, "One of these things is not like the others." When I compare and contrast the relative contribution of art, science, religion, and philosophy to the quality of life and the advancement of human prosperity, science is the clear winner. Food production and advances in the treatment of disease alone allow science to outclass the competition.

Sadly, there is something of an anti-intellectual bias against science in our culture today. The artist may take the position science fails to capture that which is most essential to our humanity. The religious may feel threatened by observations of science which seem to conflict with deeply held belief. The philosophically minded may say science distracts from the most important questions in human affairs. Art, religion, and philosophy have all witnessed the growing influence of science, and each has expressed resistance to the perceived incursion. Those who resist the contributions of science fail to recognize science merely seeks to see things as they are. Science has no agenda other than illumination. Properly understood, the resistance to science is not against science, but against reality itself.

The first principle of science is to base all claims on empirical evidence. Empirical evidence is evidence obtained through direct observation or experience. Simply put, if you want to understand the universe, LOOK! It is essential to make direct observations because things are sometimes very different from what common sense would otherwise seem to suggest. I would help my students appreciate this with a little demonstration.

Standing in front of the class holding up a psychology book and a magic maker I would ask which object they thought would hit the floor first if both were dropped at the same time. They usually assumed the heavier book would hit the floor first. It stands to reason the book would hit first. Common sense says so. Just imagine holding the two objects yourself. Anyone can tell the force exerted by gravity on the book is greater than the force on the magic marker. If I were pushing a car, the force of my pushing would be directly proportional to the speed of the car. The more force, the faster it would go. It is only natural to assume the heavier book will fall more quickly and hit the floor first. Even Aristotle believed heavier objects fall faster.

Why even pursue the matter. Some would say, "common sense tells me all I need to know. Keep your pretentious science to yourself." Let's run the experiment anyway. Here are the results; both objects accelerate at the same rate of 32 feet per second squared and hit the ground at the same time. If we factor in the book's larger size and its increased resistance to airflow during the fall, the book should actually fall more slowly, though I never detected this minor difference in any of my observations. SCIENCE!

Galileo was the first to demonstrate that objects of different weight fall at the same rate but Isaac Newton derived the mathematical formula describing gravity's behavior. He made careful observations using ramps and balls and even developed a new math to get the job done. His work enabled him to describe gravity as the attractive force between any two objects directly proportional to the product of their masses and inversely proportional to the square of the distance between them. He then realized his formula described both the movement of balls on inclined planes and the movement of planets across the heavens.

In this day and age of sensational claims and hyper-stimulating media, it is easy to become a little jaded about history. We tend to assume history to be the natural linear inevitable unfolding of events and that you or I would have done pretty much whatever needed doing if we were in the same position as the historical figure in question. Isaac Newton wrote, "In the summer of my twenty-third year I invented the calculus of flux." He needed a new mathematics to describe his observations, and so invented calculus. I don't know what you were doing in the summer of your twenty-third year, but I assure you I was nowhere near developing a new math! As far as I'm concerned, this guy was an intellectual beast.

As impressive as he was with math, his most important contribution may be the scientific method he helped pioneer. Beginning with the boomerang, invented about 17,000 years ago, on through the invention of the telescope in 1608, progress was painfully slow. Humans had the same intelligence 17,000 years ago as today but were dogged by superstition and misinformation.

Even after the introduction of the scientific method, it took centuries to move beyond our old ways of thinking. The Salem Witch Trials of 1692 were presided over by expert government judges who attempted to apply what they believed were scientific principles in their efforts to determine who was and was not a witch. This is not ancient history. In the three hundred years since, we have made remarkable progress including space travel, transplant surgery, cloning, and much more. The scientific method has earned our respect and gets much of the credit, but we are not out of the woods yet.

Even today we see climate change deniers hoping to discount the legitimate convergent findings of science. They misapply the principles of science with distortions based on non-representative data seemingly designed to obscure rather than illuminate. It is easy to imagine their skepticism being motivated by conflicts between the findings of science and deeply held beliefs or other vested interests. They proclaim the non-existence of climate change while failing to realize science is unable to prove the non-existence of anything.

The overwhelming convergent evidence for climate change is abundantly clear. Among scientists familiar with the peer reviewed research there is no controversy. Climate change is real and accelerating. Those who fail to acknowledge the reality of climate change do not understand how to rationally categorize their own observations. They do not know what it means to measure and how science allows us to draw reasonable conclusions about causation.

Measuring is comparing and contrasting observations. Some things we measure turn out to be very consistent. They show up the same way each and every time. This is especially true in the sciences we call physics and chemistry. Any gallon of water, for instance, measured at the same temperature and pressure will have the same weight as every other gallon of water at that temperature and pressure, and this is true each time we look. Similarly, any object dropped within a vacuum falls with the same acceleration as every other object dropped in a vacuum on Earth. Events happen in this way because they are governed by strict laws of nature.

Our modern understanding of these laws began about three hundred years ago. Before this, the universe was thought to operate in a "supernatural" way. Adverse events were seen as divine retribution while good fortune indicated the approval of the gods. Biology was believed to result from a mystical "élan vital" life force considered to be forever beyond human understanding. The laws of physics and chemistry now allow us a rational understanding of life, the universe and everything without the need for supernatural explanations.

Understanding naturally emerges from comparing and contrasting observations. This is a simple idea, but taken to its logical extreme; it promises a "God-like" vision of the universe. The 18th-century mathematician Laplace wrote; "We may regard the present state of the universe as the effect of its past and the cause of its future. An intellect which at a certain moment would know all forces that set nature in motion, and all positions of all items of which nature is composed, if this intellect were also vast enough to submit these data to analysis, it would embrace in a single formula the movements of the greatest bodies of the universe and those of the tiniest atom; for such an intellect nothing would be uncertain and the future just like the past would be present before its eyes."

Of course, we will never achieve the God-like vision imagined by Laplace, but we advance our understanding by using the compare and contrast methods of science. Since we can not measure the entire universe, our next best option is to measure samples taken from what researchers call populations of interest. Each sample should contain enough observations, so we have good reason to believe it represents the population we hope to understand. After designing a study intended to answer an important research question, the footwork of science begins by measuring samples from a population of interest. We then compare and contrast our measurements using the comparison tool we call statistics.

Mark Twain famously said, "There are lies, damned lies, and statistics." He was expressing a common frustration many people share due to their lack of understanding. Statistics are a powerful tool but, like all tools, they have limitations. Once you understand their limitations, you can apply them with confidence. It is easier than most people think. For us, understanding basic statistics is important because consciousness operates using the same principles.

Imagine a study looking at the effect of classroom seat location on student test performance. We want to know if sitting up front helps. There are many reasons to believe why this might be true. Signal detection theory, for instance, tells us students in the front will receive a more pure form of the lecture than students sitting in the back. The students sitting in the back will get a weaker signal due to the increased distance, and they may be distracted by students in front.

We want to control for things like eyesight and grade point average, so we randomly assign all students to their seat locations in the study. This provides greater confidence the students in front, and the students in the back will have the same overall characteristics except for the seat assigned. Random assignment reduces the chance all "A" students sit up front while all the slackers sit in the back. Okay, the seats are randomly assigned, the lecture given and the test administered.

Here are results. The six students sitting in front earned grades of 90, 90, 90, 80, 80 and 80 while the six students in back earned grades of 80, 80, 80, 70, 70, and 70. Just looking at the data, it is tempting to conclude sitting in front caused better test performance than sitting in the back. After all, the average grade for the group up front was 85 while the mean score for students in the back was 75. For the students in this study, seat location does seem to have made a difference. Let's think a little further.

We are not all that interested in the twelve students who participated in this study per se. What we really want to know is; does seat location make a difference for all students. The only way to know this would be to measure all students and compare scores. Even if we could, we still wouldn't be sure it was the seat location or some other variable responsible for group differences. So we use research design and statistics to help us get at the truth.

Here is the logic. The average score for students in front was 85, and the average score for students in the back was 75. Even if seat location had no effect at all, it would be rare for both groups to have the same exact scores. Random chance almost always produces group differences. The question then becomes this: I found a difference between groups, but is this difference within the range of differences I would expect to find due to random chance or is this difference bigger than the difference I would expect from random chance. If the difference is within the range expected due to random chance, then we say the result is not statistically significant, and the groups did not differ. If the difference between groups is bigger than the difference expected due to random chance, then we say the result is statistically significant, and the groups differed based on seat location.

The claim of statistical significance only means we have reason to believe the results represent an actual difference in the population of interest because we found a difference between groups which was bigger than the difference we would expect to find due to random chance alone. Statistical analysis of group differences provides important information. It is perhaps the most powerful tool in the social scientist's toolbox, but as you can see, it is not omnipotent.

Researchers usually set the cutoff point for statistical significance tests at five percent, meaning a one in twenty chance of being wrong. A 5 percent probability value means the difference between groups is so big it would take on average repeating the study twenty times for random chance alone to generate a difference this big assuming there is no actual difference between the groups. So statistical significance means the difference between groups is greater than the difference expected due to random chance.

For our theoretical seat location study, the group difference was statistically significant with a probability value of 0.01. A one percent probability is the same as saying the study would have to be run 100 times to find a difference this big caused by random chance alone. Because we did the study only once, we now have reason to believe seat location affects test performance in the population of interest.

Understanding how we compares groups is important because this is how we evaluate things like safety belts, public opinion polls and the effectiveness of medications. An article published in the Washington Post (Shankar Vedantam, 2002) entitled, "Against Depression, a Sugar Pill is hard to beat" found "in the majority of trials conducted by drug companies in recent decades, sugar pills have done as well as or better than antidepressants. Companies have had to conduct numerous trials to get two that show a positive result, which is the Food and Drug Administration's minimum for approval." The article stated "The makers of Prozac had to run five trials to obtain two that were positive, and the makers of Paxil and Zoloft had to run even more."

When five trials are required to get two studies with statistically significant results, we have violated the principles of statistical analysis. In effect, we are changing the probability value of the comparisons between groups. Setting the probability value at five percent for a single study will result in a one in twenty chance for a false positive result. If ten studies are done, the odds become fifty-fifty a "significant" result will emerge in the absence of any real group differences. This is no better than a coin toss. Using this flawed logic, simply doing more studies will eventually find statistically significant support for "up" being the cause of "down." This perversion of science not only harms patients; it contributes to the skepticism toward science undermining our entire society. Education is the answer. Buy another copy of this book; it makes a great gift.

Nature operates with a flawless efficiency and consciousness is a natural process. So it makes sense the scientific method and the tools of statistical analysis mirror the process of consciousness itself. We see the same dynamic, transitional and relational process taking place between clusters of neurons in the brain "voting" on the context of experience as occurs with observations in a study "voting" on the effectiveness of antidepressant medication. Both scientific inquiry and consciousness sample reality, assess similarities and differences, and generate theories of causation. And so, the compare and contrast methods of science helps us understand the nature of consciousness. As my teacher once said about compare and contrast, "well that is all there is."

JOANNE LEE (2011) Applied Psycholinguistics Volume 32, Issue 1 January 2011, pp. 69-92 Size matters: Early vocabulary as a predictor of language and literacy competence.

Shankar Vedantam (2002), The Washington Post May 7, 2002, Against Depression, a Sugar Pill Is Hard to Beat

2 THE BEGINNINGS OF CONSCIOUSNESS

Establishing a framework for describing consciousness is a challenge. It seems no matter where we start, it feels like we are starting in the middle. For this reason. do not be too concerned if you find the next few chapters challenging. This just means you are paying attention. Read with a sense of adventure, and as you gain a more global understanding, the gaps will naturally fill in. Enjoy!

Consciousness is a naturally emergent process. It emerges from the dynamic associations between the elements of nature. So understanding consciousness requires understanding of the associations of natural systems. There is no better place to start than to recognize that nature is extremely intelligent and supremely efficient at maximizing survival. Traits, such as consciousness, are selected by nature for the purpose of advancing survival.

Now a precise definition for the word "consciousness" is hard to pin down. The word most often used as a synonym for the word consciousness is the word "awareness." However, these two words are not equivalent. To be aware is somehow more basic than to be conscious. Someone might consider a thermostat aware of room temperature, but few would say a thermostat is conscious of anything.

One reason consciousness is hard to define is that it cannot be measured directly. In fact, the only way to detect the consciousness of others is through their behavior. Even if a machine could be made to measure the consciousness of others directly, the only way to read the machine's output would be through the observation of the machine's behavior thereby leading to an infinite regress. The consciousness of others can only be measured through behavior.

Consciousness, like understanding, is a process. To describe something as a process is to draw attention to the sequence of events making up the steps in the process. Understanding consciousness, therefore, requires understanding the dynamic, transitional and relational events inducing the behaviors suggesting the presence of consciousness. So our search for the earliest beginnings of consciousness in nature will start with a look at the events inducing the intelligent behavior of simple organisms.

Plants have "awareness" of their environment as demonstrated by their ability to grow towards the light. This is called heliotropism. There must be some awareness of the environment for plants to act in this way. Some species of plants have heliotropic flowers which follow the sun's motion across the sky during the day and then assume a more random orientation at night.

This behavior occurs through the action of specialized motor cells located in the flexible segment near the base of the flower called the pulvinus. These motor cells pump potassium ion solution into nearby tissues changing the fluid pressure within. The pulvinus flexes as the engorged motor cells on the shadow side become elongated under pressure pointing the flower towards the sun. The behavior is intelligent because it facilitates pollination by increasing the flower's visibility to pollinating insects.

Plants also show awareness when responding to insect attack by increasing production of defensive chemicals making them less palatable to insects. Interestingly, some plants can sense the defensive chemicals of their neighbors and will ramp up their own defenses even before being attacked themselves. Here we see the barest beginnings of a consciousness enabling groups of plants to adapt to the environment better than individuals alone. When associated into groups increased consciousness naturally emerges as demonstrated by the ability to anticipate and prepare for attack.

The behavior of each plant is reflexive based on cause and effect rules of chemistry and physics. Insect attack just equals increased chemical production. Similarly, detection of increased defensive chemicals in others just equals increased defensive chemical production in self. Following these simple rules, plants in groups express greater intelligence and awareness than individuals alone. Together, they form a network of association. Through this association, we see the emergence of the beginnings of something like consciousness.

Plant networks do not have the fixed associations of a developed nervous system. Instead, they associate with each other via chemicals wafted in the air. This is similar to the way neurotransmitters communicate across the synapse between the neurons of an integrated nervous system. Even with these very loose associations, plant networks demonstrate intelligence approaching something like consciousness. Of course, most people would not consider a meadow of plants to have anything like "real" consciousness, but who can deny the emergence of increased intelligence?

Single-celled microorganisms also have an awareness of the environment enabling them to move about seeking nutrients and avoiding adverse conditions. As with plants, the bacteria behave in reflexive ways, and like the plants, when associated into groups, we see the emergence of increased intelligence.

Though the microbes do not "learn" new behaviors, the colony as a whole responds to the environment in intelligently adaptive ways. The mechanism by which the colony adapts is survival itself. This adaptation process is also a form of emergent consciousness. The colony is more than the sum of its parts. We can see this playing out in the transformation of the Staphylococcus Aureus bacteria.

Staphylococcus Aureus is a bacterium commonly found throughout the human body. It lives on the skin, in the airways, and throughout the digestive tract. We are host to many such microorganisms which for us usually promote health. Collectively, they are called normal flora. Normal flora helps us stay healthy by competing with pathogens for space and nutrients, by producing compounds which kill harmful bacteria, by providing essential vitamins which we are unable to make (e.g. vitamin B12), by boosting the immune system and by helping us digest our food.

In 1923, upon returning to his laboratory after a vacation, Alexander Fleming noticed some old bread covered with colonies of mold and bacteria. He saw areas adjacent to the mold with no bacterial growth. Fleming realized the mold had a way of inhibiting the bacteria's incursion. He went on to isolate the compound inhibiting the bacteria and so discovered penicillin. Before the discovery of antibiotics less than a hundred years ago, a simple staph infection or strep throat could easily kill. Today, we often don't even slow down. But the bacteria are learning!

Life itself is a dynamic, transitional and relational process and evolution is ongoing. All species alive today are perfectly evolved for the environments in which they developed, and all species are also in transition. Properly understood, the bacteria are not aspiring to someday become human if only they play their cards right. Rather, they are ideally suited for the particular niche in the environment in which they develop in an ongoing adaptive way. As part of this ability to adapt, the bacteria are becoming resistant to antibiotics.

Individual bacteria are not genetically identical. Some, due to random variation, are more likely to be naturally resistant to antibiotics than others. Antibiotics tend to kill the most susceptible bacteria first. Those with greater natural immunity to an antibiotic will tend to survive longer. Antibiotic therapy rarely kills all infecting bacteria, so resistance will naturally emerge with regular antibiotic usage.

The process is accelerated when antibiotics are misused. People are naturally motivated to misuse their antibiotics because going to the doctor and pharmacy is both expensive and time-consuming. Patients are therefore motivated to save any "extra" antibiotic for their next infection when their symptoms abate. Symptoms usually resolve well before all infecting bacteria die. Since the most susceptible bacteria die first, the surviving bacteria will have increased resistance to the antibiotic. Over time this has resulted in strains of bacteria known as "Superbugs."

The superbug Methicillin-Resistant Staphylococcus Aureus (MRSA) is a scourge of the health care industry. MRSA is one of the dramatic flesh eating bacteria seen in the news, and there are fewer and fewer antibiotics which can kill it. Staphylococcus Aureus has adapted to its environment. With no fixed association between the bacteria, there is no consciousness in the conventional sense of the word. Even so, the MRSA bacteria intelligently adapts when associated into networks or groups.

So we see the emergence of intelligence in the simplest of organisms exhibiting the most basic reflexive behaviors when joined together into loosely associated networks. Both plants and bacteria express their "will to survive" as evidenced by growing towards the light or moving towards sustenance. This intelligence leaps forward when organisms become associated into networks or groups. Groups of plants adjust their chemistry in anticipation of attack and colonies of bacteria alter their DNA in response to a chemical assault. Groups are naturally more intelligent than individuals.

The common denominator is actions favoring survival. Thier reflex responses are the natural outcome of the physics and chemistries involved. For the behaviors to increase survival, they must be in response to the signals of the environment. This stimulus and response association is the root of the survival instinct inherent to all life. It is the earliest beginnings of the "will." The "will" in the purest form just is the survival instinct based on physics, chemistry, and probability.

Chemotaxis is the movement of microbes in response to the chemistry of the environment. Some bacteria move towards favorable chemistry like glucose and away from harmful chemicals such as phenol by using a tail-like structure called a flagellum. The flagellum plays a critical role in the development of almost all animal life on Earth. It is the flagellum which propels the sperm towards the egg during fertilization and it is chemistry which dictates the behavior.

Flagellum appear to wag back and forth, but in fact, the corkscrew shaped structures actually spin like tiny rotary motors. They are able spin in both directions. Counter-clockwise rotation aligns the fibers which make up the tail into a single corkscrew shaped bundle causing the bacteria to move forward. Clockwise rotation causes the fibers to unbundle making the bacterium tumble randomly.

The direction of rotation depends on the chemistry of the environment. Life affirming chemistry results in forward motion. Aversive chemistry results in intermittent random tumbling to change direction. These two behaviors are an early expression of a "choice" emerging from a single organism. The organism is saying through behavior; "I like this better than that."

With the two different motion variables of chemotaxis, we see the emergence of increased intelligence from a network of associations all contained within a single organism. The network of associations allowing chemotaxis behavior is between the chemistry sensing units and variable motor response units. Like a meadow of plants or a colony of bacteria, we see the emergence of increased intelligence with networked associations. With chemotaxis the network of association is all contained within a single organism.

Individual plant behavior was limited to increase chemical production or no increase chemical production. Similarly, MRSA bacteria adaptation was restricted to survive or perish. These are simple "on or off" responses. With chemotaxis, we see something new. We still have the "on or off" option for motion or no motion, but now we have a new variable; rotate clockwise or rotate counterclockwise. In effect, the bacteria have the ability to pause, advance or retreat from the environment. This new network of responses allows for the emergence of increased intelligence signaling a significant step forward in the barest beginnings of consciousness. It is interesting to note that the same three responses pioneered by the microorganisms; pause, advance, retreat, apply throughout the rest of nature.

These behaviors suggesting consciousness emerge from the dynamic, transitional and relational associations between the structures having the conscious experience. The cascading sequence of signals occurring between structures inducing the behaviors result from the chemistry and physics of the interaction. As these systems reflexively obey the immutable laws of chemistry and physics consciousness emerges.

Intelligent behavior does not exist in a vacuum; it only exists relative to the context of an environment. When actions are limited to "motion" or "no motion," it is the environment acting on the organism. The situation dictates the outcome, which is just another way of saying there is no evidence for "real" consciousness. When a third potential variable becomes operative, rotate clockwise, rotate counter clockwise, or no rotation at all, we see an increased opportunity for the emergence of intelligence because now, for the first time, the organism appears to be acting upon the environment.

So, we see the emergence of increased intelligence when plants or bacteria become networked together following the simple rules of chemistry and physics. These loosely associated networks induce a simple form of consciousness able to adapt to the environment intelligently. The next step in the development of consciousness occurs as individual organisms develop the capacity to "choose" between behavioral responses based on self-contained networks of association.

The evidence for consciousness is intelligent behavior and behavior is intelligent when it increases survival. As such, consciousness is always a relational process between the organism and the environment. It is always context driven. Individual consciousness begins when intelligent behavior relative to the environment emerges from networked associations between structures contained within a single organism. Said another way, consciousness emerges from the network of connections between structures within an organism as the organism networks with the environment. Consciousness is an emergent property of networks of networks.

The entire universe is hinged together through association networks. Intelligence emerges by virtue of these connections. This process of emergent intelligence taps into the same mechanism expressed by the association of variable in probability statistics. It should come as no surprise statistics plays such a significant role in our understanding of the universe. Statistics "work" because they model and reflect the universe accurately.

The most accurate assessment of reality comes from the sampling of multiple imperfect observations and averaging the results. These group observations converge to provide increased confidence in the assessment. Physical reality, like consciousness, is dynamic, transitional and relational. No single observation is capable of capturing the fully dynamic, transitional, and relational context of a moving target. So we use multiple observations averaged together to see things more clearly. This process works because groups of plants, groups of microbes and even groups of neurons in the human brain express a context driven emergent intelligence based on the principle of statistics described as the "wisdom of the crowd."

The "wisdom of the crowd" is a phrase referring to the increased accuracy seen when groups of independent observations collectively "vote" on the nature of reality by sampling and averaging multiple independent observations. The classic example occurred back in 1906 at a country fair in Plymouth Massachusetts.

A contest was held to guess the weight of a slaughtered and dressed ox. Some eight hundred people participated including several expert cattlemen. Statistician Francis Galton gathered the estimates and found the median guess of 1207 pounds to be accurate to within 1% of the actual weight of 1198 lbs. This group estimate was more accurate than any of the individual estimates including those of the expert cattlemen.

The theory behind the process goes something like this: All observations tend to include some level of error or "statistical noise" within the measurement. When groups of independent observations are sampled and averaged together, these cumulative random errors tend to cancel each other out in such a way that the group average tends to be more accurate than the individual observations. In essence, each observation is probably "wrong," but each tends to be "wrong" in a different way because there are many more ways to be wrong than to be right. Averaging groups of independent observations tends to cancel out the "wrong" while leaving in more of the "right." These groups of observations are combined to create a probability distribution with the average approximating the true value of the quantity being estimated.

Consciousness is a context-driven dynamic, transitional, and relational process. In multicellular organisms, the relations are between the cells making up the organism. The possibility for anything like human consciousness begins with the development of a complex multicellular nervous system. The Individual neurons within a complex nervous system have no more consciousness than the individual bacteria of a colony. Just as colonies of bacteria express emergent intelligence through association, so too do groups of neurons within a nervous system.

When groups of bacteria or groups of plants join together and follow the reflexive rules of survival, we see the emergence of a rudimentary form of consciousness able to adapt to the environment. A similar process plays out in the nervous systems of more complex organisms as groups of neurons follow the reflexive rules of neuron behavior to induce emergent consciousness. As the complexity of neural networks increases, the resolution of awareness also increases.

We have indeed come a long way. In just a few short pages we have described the emergence of simple consciousness in the natural world. Before going further, however, we need to build a foundation for the new structure of our understanding. There are a few subjects we must cover in order to provide a context for the new information. Some of these topics may at first seem unrelated to the task at hand, but there is a good reason for their inclusion. In fact, the structure of this book mirrors the structure of consciousness. Each chapter is a necessary dynamic, transitional and relational component required for understanding. If it is not clear to you why I have included a section, it just means you still do not understand the nature of consciousness. Understanding the structure of this book is equivalent to understanding consciousness.

I like to think of this chapter as being something like the appetizer for a fine meal. I hope it has generated a hunger in you for more understanding. Here is the rest of the menu; Chapter three takes a brief look at the hardware of human consciousness, the nervous system. Chapter four describes the survival based motivational operating systems of reflex, instinct, and instinctively motivated drives. Chapter five covers association and learning, and Chapter six outlines dissociation and attention.

These early chapters describe the conditions necessary for simple forms of consciousness to come into being. They account for the consciousness of organisms ranging from plants and microbes on up through worms and fish. Understanding how these systems operate allows us to see how the same principles apply to more complex systems of consciousness.

When dissociation joins the discussion, we begin to see circularity in the language used to describe consciousness.

The words used at this stage in the discourse do not connect well with the rest of common language. Words like conscious, aware, spirit, mind and soul are all used to define each other, but none of these words easily hinges on concepts outside of this somehow mysterious island of descriptors. This is a reflection of our difficulty understanding consciousness. There is one notable exception.

The bridge to deeper understanding is the concept "information." Consciousness is composed of thought and thought consists of information. To understand consciousness then, we must understand the way information is processed. Chapter seven describes the signal transfer process we call communication. Chapter eight follows the signals of communication from sensation on to perception. Chapter nine examines the development of language, and Chapter Ten presents a model of cascading signal transfer as the inducer of human conscious experience. Chapter eleven then describes the cauldron-like nature of the signal transfer process which induces human consciousness.

The final chapter acknowledges signal transfer to be the universal process of association in the cosmos inducing both mind and matter leading to some surprising realizations about the nature of self-concept and free will. Understanding dynamic, transitional and relational signal transfer just is the awakening to the nature of consciousness, the universe and everything.

3 THE NERVOUS SYSTEM

To understand human consciousness we need to understand the systems upon which human consciousness is most directly dependent. Learning about the nervous system not only offers insight into the nature of consciousness, it also suggests the best practices for developing and maintaining good mental health. Just as a physical therapist must understand the form and function of the musculoskeletal system to recognize conditions of the body, we must understand the workings of the nervous system to appreciate conditions of the mind.

Now, the distinction between the "physical" and the "mental" is not at all clear. Philosophers have wrestled with these ideas since time out of memory. Monism, the philosophical view that there is nothing over and above physical reality, takes the position the universe is made up of only one kind of stuff, and that stuff is physical. In contrast, "Dualism" takes the position that a non-physical mind exists apart from the rest of physical reality. Though the debate continues, the nervous system is clearly a physical structure, and all reliable evidence indicates mind and body are inexorably connected.

People speak of "the mental" with terms like "spirit," "mind" and "soul" as if they could exist independent of the body, but there is no reliable evidence for the existence of mind without a body. The mind, if it exists, almost surely resides within the body.

The properties of a system emerge from the associations between elements making up the system. Biology is an emergent property of the laws of chemistry which, in turn, can be seen as an emergent property of the laws of particle physics. Similarly, consciousness can be thought of as an emergent property of neurobiology just as psychology is an emergent property of consciousness. At the next level up, both culture and free-market economic theories are emergent properties of psychology. And so it goes, everything hinges upon everything else for its dynamic, transitional and relational coherence. We study the nervous system because human consciousness emerges most directly from the properties of human neurobiology.

The most prominent feature of the nervous system is the brain. The human brain is made up of about one hundred billion neurons. These interconnected nerve cells function like tiny on and off switches which flash on only briefly when activated. Consciousness emerges from the signal transfer patterns between clusters of neurons. Earlier we noted how the signal transfer patterns between groups of plants and groups of microbes allowed for the emergence of intelligence. A similar process takes place with the signal transfer patterns between neurons in the brain. To see how it all works, let's begin by looking at the structure of a typical nerve cell.

Nerve cells have three basic parts; a cell body, dendrites, and axons. If you have never seen a nerve cell, just imagine a young plant seedling. The root system represents the dendrites, the central seed simulates the cell body, and the sprout approximates the axon. Different types of nerve cells have different configurations of dendrites and axons and use different neurotransmitters.

Nerve cells are grouped into three broad categories called afferent neurons, efferent neurons and interneurons. Afferent neurons receive signals from the sensory organ systems; efferent nerve cells send signals to organs, muscles, and glands, and interneurons send and receive messages to and from other nerve cells.

Nerve cells are in the business of signal processing. The

dendrite receives the signal, and the axon transmits the signal. The signals are conveyed across the cell body by changes in the cell membrane's permeability to electrolytes in a cascading domino-like fashion with an electrochemical quality. We can actually measure the electrical activity of neurons by placing electrodes on the scalp in the same way we measure the electrical activity of heart cells by placing electrodes on the chest.

Nerve cells fire in an all-or-nothing fashion. If a signal is strong enough, the cell fires completely. If the signal falls below a minimum threshold, the cell doesn't fire at all. Both muscle cells and nerve cells work in this all or nothing sort of way. When a cell fires it is called depolarization. After depolarization, the cell must make itself ready to fire again. This is called repolarization. Depolarization and repolarization cycles can happen very fast especially if the distance to be covered is small. A hummingbird's heart rate can exceed 1,000 beats per minute.

Nerve cells don't touch other cells as they send and receive signals. Instead, they communicate via chemical messengers released at the very small junction between cells called the synapse. These chemical messengers are called neurotransmitters. There are over a hundred different neurotransmitters identified so far but, ten of them do over 90% of the work. Some neurotransmitter systems are well understood, but understanding of the system as a whole is far from complete.

So nerve cells send and receive signals like tiny on and off switches which flash on only briefly when fired. They send and receive their messages via neurotransmitters released at the synapse. Now that we have a basic understanding of nerve cells, we can look at the way groups of nerves cells join together to make up the systems and subsystems of the nervous system.

The nervous system is usually considered to be the command and control center of the body; however, communication between the body and the nervous system occurs in both directions. The nervous system influences the body as the body influences the nervous system. There are many feedback loops which fine-tune the system for optimal performance under changing conditions.

For instance, whenever an organism perceives a significant threat, the adrenal glands located just above the kidneys release a hormone called adrenaline dramatically increasing both physiological and psychological arousal. Recall that it was the nervous system's perception of threat that triggered the adrenal glands in the first place. So the system is feeding back on itself. In a similar but less immediate way, testosterone is a hormone influencing aggression. Aggressive behavior, in turn, affects the level of testosterone produced. The distinction between the brain and body is not as absolute as many believe because both the brain and the body have "awareness" and each influences the other.

The human nervous system has two main parts, the central nervous system, and the peripheral nervous system. The central nervous system includes the brain and the spinal cord which are located toward the center of the body, while the peripheral nervous system connects the central nervous system out to the periphery.

The peripheral nervous system has two subsystems called the somatic nervous system and the autonomic nervous system. The somatic nervous connects the brain to the voluntary skeletal muscles while the autonomic nervous system regulates heart rate, respiratory rate, digestion, blood pressure, and more. Though called involuntary, voluntary control of autonomic functions is possible with mindfulness and biofeedback training.

The autonomic nervous system also has two subsystems called the sympathetic and parasympathetic nervous systems. These two systems work in dynamic opposition to each other to control heart rate, blood pressure, airway tone, pupil dilation, and digestion. Stimulate the sympathetic nervous system and heart rate goes up. Stimulate the parasympathetic nervous system, and heart rate goes down. Conversely, inhibit the sympathetic nervous system and heart rate goes down while inhibiting the parasympathetic nervous system causes the heart rate to increase.

Nature is extremely intelligent and supremely efficient. It is no accident polar bears have thick white fur. Polar bears have thick white fur because thick white fur offers the greatest survival advantage for the environment in which the polar bear developed. Thick white fur enables the bear to keep warm while stealthily hunting prey in snowy conditions.

Three and a half billion years of trial and error have produced some remarkable efficiencies. All creatures have been designed to maximize survival within the environments in which they developed. Characteristics increasing survival are more likely to be passed on, so from this Darwinian perspective, we can deduce how the autonomic nervous system regulates body functions.

To do so, let's run through a little thought experiment. I want you to imagine a tiger just walked into the room. No, not good enough. I want you to really "experience" the beast, I want you to feel its hot breath change the atmosphere of the room, to draw the tiger's presence fully into your consciousness. Let's get graphic.

The tiger is the largest cat species alive weighing in at up to 700 pounds with a body length of 12 feet, not including the tail. It is the third largest land carnivore behind only the polar bear and the brown bear. Its most recognizable feature is a pattern of dark vertical stripes on a background of reddish-orange fur becoming lighter towards the underside. It has exceptionally stout teeth with the longest canines of all land animals with a crown height of 3.5 inches. When standing on all fours, they are almost as tall as the average human. They have incredible agility powered by muscles like ribbons of steel.

Two men are walking together in the forest. One says to the other, "There are tigers around here. What are you going to do if we see a tiger?" The other replies "If I see a tiger, I'm going to run." The first man says, "You can't outrun a tiger." The second man quips, "I don't need to outrun the tiger, I only need to outrun you!" Though a cute little story, there is not much truth to it because from the tiger's perspective; there is no uncertainty about the kill at all. The tiger will have whomever the tiger wants. We are talking about power and agility far beyond the range of ordinary human experience.

So, what kind of survival-enhancing physiologic reactions should we expect from an encounter with a threat like this? Remember, the autonomic nervous system consists of the sympathetic and parasympathetic systems dynamically balancing heart rate, blood pressure, respiratory rate, airway tone, pupil dilation, and digestion. Under severe threat, the sympathetic branch becomes more activated dramatically increases arousal. This is called the "fight or flight" response. Think of the sensation you experienced the last time you were almost in a car accident, or on a roller coaster, or looking down the barrel of a gun. These are the types of experiences which tend to induce a "fight or flight" response.

Okay, tiger standing in the doorway; heart rate, respiratory rate and blood pressure all increase to provide the skeletal muscles what they need most, blood flow and oxygen for maximum performance. In contrast, the smooth muscle tissue regulating airway tone relaxes causing the bronchioles to dilate allowing more oxygen to enter the bloodstream. This also has the effect of reducing the noise of breathing lessening the chance of being detected while at the same time enhancing hearing. The nares flair open increasing the sense of smell and the pupils dilate allowing more light onto the retina for maximum visual acuity.

The liver is kicking out glucose (fuel) as fast as it can, but digestion itself has shut down. Dry mouth occurs because salvation is part of digestion. Absorbing the nutrients from last night's dinner is now a low priority. In fact, the weight of the meal in the bowel may even be a liability. If you have ever picked up a hamster only to find a little something deposited in your hand after you put it back down, you have witnessed sympathetic activation. There really is something to the phrase "scared the crap out of me." When this happens, the organism increases the chance of escape by reducing body weight, and changes to the environment may distract or discourage certain threats.

This adrenaline fueled state also changes the way information is processed in the brain. During periods of extreme stress, people experience what seems to be a slowing down of time with an ultra fine perception of the details surrounding the unfolding experience. Research using high-speed alphanumeric displays placed on the wrist and viewed during periods of extreme stress (being dropped backward from a platform 150 feet in the air) suggest perception does not actually speed up (Stetson C, Fiesta MP, Eagleman DM, 2007). Stressed subjects could not read the rapidly changing alphanumeric display any faster than non-stressed subjects. Instead, the illusion of time slowing down is thought to result from inhibition of sensory filters usually limiting the volume of information allowed into active attention. Real-time information processing increases by throwing open the floodgates of signal detection. The system will sort out the overflow data later if there is a later.

Because the sympathetic and the parasympathetic systems operate in opposition to each other, just reverse the responses of sympathetic activation to describe parasympathetic activation. Stimulate the parasympathetic nervous system, and you get decreased heart rate, decreased respiratory rate, decreased blood pressure, increased bronchial tone and increased pupil constriction.

Understanding the way the system operates allows us to treat conditions with drugs which stimulate or inhibit the subsystems of the autonomic nervous system. Asthma, for instance, is characterized by airway constriction and inflammation. If during an asthma attack, a tiger were to walk into the room, sympathetic activation would likely result in airway dilation and symptom relief. We don't like the side effects of this treatment (being eaten), so instead, we give medications which stimulate the sympathetic nervous system in the same way a tiger threat would. Albuterol is a drug categorized as sympathomimetic because it mimics activation of the sympathetic nervous system. We can now understand and even predict the side effects of these drugs, such as upset stomach and increased heart rate because these symptoms also accompany sympathetic activation.

The Belladonna plant (beautiful lady) has a long history of use as a medicine, a cosmetic, and even a poison. European women of the seventeenth century used extracts from the plant to make a tea which induced pupil dilation. Pupils dilate during sexual arousal indicating a readiness to mate. Dilated pupils are generally considered a sign of beauty giving the Belladonna plant its name.

Atropine is the active ingredient in the belladonna plant, and it is still in wide medical use today. Atropine works by inhibiting the parasympathetic nervous system. Think of the sympathetic and parasympathetic systems working like a balance scale. The scale tilts towards pupil dilation by stimulating (adding weight) to the sympathetic side or by inhibiting (removing weight) from the parasympathetic side. Atropine works by removing weight from the parasympathetic side of the scale. So we see the same pupil dilation during both sympathetic activation and parasympathetic inhibition. Atropine is in the class of drugs called parasympatholytic because it inhibits the parasympathetic nervous system.

So far we have looked at the way nerve cells send and receive signals followed by a brief look at the somatic and autonomic subsystems of the peripheral nervous system. We will now turn our attention to the central nervous system.

The central nervous system is made up of the spinal cord and the brain. The spinal cord is a remarkable structure. It is made up of nerves which pass through the vertebrae facilitating communication between the brain and the body. Early in the development of life on Earth nature decided spinal cords were a good idea because almost all animals have one. Yes, there are insects and mollusks with fundamentally different designs, but once we get to worms and fish on up through amphibians, reptiles, birds, and mammals it's spinal cords all the way, and they are all remarkably alike.

You can remember the number of vertebrae in your spine by thinking of the time people usually eat meals. Breakfast is at seven, and there are seven cervical or neck vertebrae. Lunch is at twelve, and there are twelve thoracic vertebrae. These are the ones with ribs attached. Dinner is at five corresponding to the five lumbar vertebrae of the lower back. There are also five fused vertebrae making up the sacrum and a small tail section composed of several fused vertebrae.

Just for fun, guess how many cervical vertebrae a puppy has. That's right, seven. How about an elephant? Yep, seven. What about a giraffe? Seven again. Okay, how about a whale? Just as Darwin's theory would predict, seven; another little piece of convergent evidence supporting the overwhelmingly well-supported idea that natural selection is the way life developed on Earth. It all just makes sense. There are advantages to having a good central processing system, and once a good design emerges, that design tends to get passed along.

The spinal cord not only transmits signals between the brain and the body; it also performs some basic information processing itself. Many reflexes occur at the level of the spinal cord. Let's say you accidentally put your hand on a hot stove. In response, the pain receptors in your hand will send a signal through the nerves in your arm across your shoulder to the spinal cord. Here two things happen at roughly the same time. The message continues on up to the brain where higher level information processing takes place, and you may begin to think to yourself "Hey, my hand is in big trouble."

Fortunately, while you were wasting precious time telling yourself the obvious, the spinal cord already took action. In fact, the immediate danger probably passed even before you fully realized you had a problem, because as the pain signal made its way to the spinal cord and started toward the brain, a second signal was simultaneously routed back down from the spinal cord to the shoulder and arm causing the bicep muscle group to aggressively contract thereby pulling the hand out of danger. There are many such reflexes built into the system. Even with this robust emergency response significant damage occurs. Think how much worse it would be if our response depended upon processing in the brain before reacting.

Worms have a simple nervous system with a brain and spinal cord like structures. As the complexity of life increases so too does the complexity of the nervous system. If you compare the anatomies of creatures from the very simple on up to the more complex, it becomes apparent new structures get added onto existing simpler designs. Efficient structures once established tend to stay, and they tend to perform the same functions across species. It all strongly suggests an evolutionary process at work.

As we move up the spinal cord toward the brain, the complexity of signal processing increases. Upon entering the base of the skull, the spinal cord thickens and becomes the medulla oblongata and the pons. These lower level brainstem structures deal primarily with the regulation of our most basic vital metabolic functions such as sleep, respiration, swallowing, digestion, bladder control, equilibrium, and posture; what all creatures need to manage their physiology.

There is a structure just behind the brainstem called the cerebellum (Latin for little brain) which plays a role in fine motor coordination. The cerebellum makes up about thirty percent of a fish brain suggesting the relative importance of this structure for balance and control in these nimble creatures. Fish exhibit amazing agility and coordination in groups where schools can appear to move like a single organism.

Just above the pons and the medulla, we find the hypothalamus which regulates sleep cycles, hunger, thirst, hormone release, and more. The thalamus (just above the hypothalamus) is involved in relaying sensory and motor information to and from higher levels of the brain acting as a sort of information gatekeeper. Other important structures in this region include the hippocampus, which is involved with spatial memory, memory storage, and navigation; and the amygdala associated with our most primitive emotions and emotional memory. Each of these specialized clusters of neurons performs specialized functions contributing their signal transfer patterns to the ongoing stream of unfolding consciousness.

The hippocampus contains a group of specialized neurons called grid cells. Grid cells allow the organism to stay spatially oriented to the environment. John M. O'Keefe, Dr. May-Britt Moser, and Dr. Edvard I. Moser received a Nobel Prize in 2014 for their discovery of the way grid cells allow cognitive mapping of the environment in the brain. The cells are laid out in an equidistant grid-like pattern allowing the organism to map the environment onto the grid of equilateral triangles. Moser, Kropff, and May-Britt Moser (2008) conducted experiments on rats demonstrating how grid cells are differentially activated as the rat traverses the environment.

There are many specialized clusters of neurons in the brain configured into many specialized neural networks. Each specialized network of cells performs at least one specialized function expressing at least one facet of a context specific awareness. No one has a complete understanding of all aspects of awareness in the brain, or the ways these systems interact to induce consciousness. In our brief tour so far we have touched on systems producing reflex awareness, sympathetic awareness, parasympathetic awareness and grid cell spatial orientation awareness. The list goes on and on.

The structures we have described so far represent the

most primitive parts of the human brain. If we look at an alligator's brain, we see many of the same structures performing many of the same functions. The human brain has many more structures than the alligator brain, but the structures described so far constitute pretty much the entire reptilian brain.

This is the seat of our most primitive emotions. These emotions, like everything else, developed to advance survival. It is the primary function of emotion to motivate behavior. Primal emotions are clarion calls for action. It is easy to underestimate the power of these emotions while comfortably sitting back reading a book. Keep in mind evolution has placed these primitive emotions right alongside our most vital physiologic functions such as heart rate, respiratory rate, and blood pressure. These are the functions upon which life depends and so emotion emerging from this region of the brain can seem as important as life itself. Is it any wonder we sometimes have difficulty controlling our emotions.

To understand the way primitive emotions influence our behavior, let's first consider how they play out in the alligator. The alligator brain has the same structures as the lower levels of the human brain without all that messy language and rationalization stuff on top. Let's take a look at the full range of emotions in the life of an alligator.

An alligator has four basic emotions. The first emotional state is just sitting around being an alligator, sunshine and flies. State number two, "I will rip you to shreds and swallow you." The human analog is anger. State number three, "oh crap, something is going to rip me to shreds and swallow me." The human analog here is fear. And state number four, "Hey baby how about we make some more alligators." Here, the analog is lust.

Anger, fear, and lust are the most powerful human

emotions, and now we can see why. They originate from the same area of the brain which also regulates our most basic vital physiologic functions. They can appear to be as important as life itself. And just as with the alligator, when these emotions arise in us, they tend to induce behavior. Also, because the anger, fear and lust structures are immediately adjacent to one another, and because nervous tissue is excitable, when one area becomes activated, the other nearby areas also tend to become activated. This goes a long way toward explaining the aggressive "who's your daddy" energy sometimes seen in the heat of romantic passion.

For the alligator, these powerful emotions have contributed to a long history of success. Just look at the record. It's been working pretty well for over 65 million years. When we experience these primitive emotions, our higher brain functions can become blocked. Drugs and alcohol also tend to knock out the higher functions first, leaving the alligator in charge, and so we see why these altered states of consciousness are often associated with violent antisocial behavior. According to the U.S. Department of Justice, thirty-six percent of convicted felons reported drinking alcohol at the time of their offense. Alligators don't do well in society.

The structures located above the alligator brain are collectively called the cerebral cortex. This area is what most people think of when they think "brain." The cerebral cortex has a left and a right hemisphere and each hemisphere has four lobes. The cortex is responsible for memory, attention, perceptual awareness, thought, language and what most people think of as consciousness.

The left hemisphere controls the right side of the body, and the right hemisphere controls the left. Some of the functions of the hemispheres are mirrored, such as sensory perception and motor control, while other functions are not, such as language processing.

The cortex is made up of gray matter composed of nerve cell bodies and unmyelinated fibers surrounding the deeper white matter made of myelinated axons. Myelin is the fatty insulating sheath surrounding axons increasing the speed and efficiency of impulse conduction.

The surface of the cortex is smooth in rodents and other small mammals, but in larger mammals and primates it has deep grooves (sulci) and wrinkles (gyri). These folds increase the surface area beyond what would otherwise fit within the skull. More surface area equals more processing power. All human brains have the same overall pattern of gyri and sulci, though individuals differ in detail.

The two lobes at the back of the cortex are called the occipital lobes. They are primarily involved in visual information processing. Humans are very visual creatures in that we perceive and understand the world largely through visual signals. Dogs, on the other hand, perceive and understand the world more through their sense of smell. So it makes sense human occipital lobes are proportionally larger than dog occipital lobes. We will explore visual processing in greater detail in later chapters.

Just in front of the occipital lobes making up the lower center portion of the cerebral cortex are the temporal lobes. The temporal lobes contain the primary auditory cortex which receives signals from the ear. The temporal lobes are also involved in the retention of visual memories and the processing of combined visual, auditory and tactile sensory input. Wernicke's area of the left temporal lobe is associated with comprehending language and deriving semantic meaning.

The parietal lobes are located above the temporal lobes. They are primarily involved in our tactile and spatial information processing. Signals from the skin pass up through the spinal cord through the thalamus and then on to the parietal lobes where the information gets integrated into the visual processing system enabling the parietal cortex to map objects onto body coordinate positions. This makes walking on uneven terrain easy which sounds simple, but try getting a robot to do it.

The strip of the brain located at the front of each parietal lobe is called the primary somatosensory cortex. This prominent structure is the main processing center for the sense of touch. Every tactile sensory nerve from the tip of your toes to the top of your head connects to your brain here. In keeping with nature's penchant for efficiency, the torso has relatively few nerves per square inch while the face, mouth, and hands have many more nerves for a given area. More nerves mean higher resolution and more detailed sensory information. The somatosensory cortex is where the skin meets the brain.

The frontal lobes are adjacent to the parietal lobes and above the temporal lobes. They seem to have an executive awareness function associated with consciousness and identity. It is here we recognize the consequences of our actions allowing us to override the alligator brain for more socially acceptable behaviors. It is largely in the frontal lobes where we experience conscious awareness of the similarities and differences between things. The frontal lobes play a significant role in the retention of long-term memories and their associated emotions.

The left frontal lobe has a specialized region adjacent to the temporal lobe called Broca's area that is responsible for generating speech. When someone has a stroke and loses their ability to speak, it is often damage to Broca's area or associated structures responsible for the impaired speech. Speech processing is often both a visual and an auditory signal processing function. It is Wernicke's area in the temporal lobe in combination with Broca's area of the frontal lobe where sight and sound combine to derive meaning.

The frontal lobes also contain many of the dopamine-sensitive neurons located in the brain. The dopamine neurotransmitter system has been associated with reward, attention, short-term memory, planning, and motivation. It plays a significant role in all reward-motivated behavior. Every type of reward studied has been found to increase the action of dopamine in the brain. Addictive drugs, such as cocaine, amphetamine and methamphetamine amplify the effects of dopamine, and personality traits such as extroversion and reward seeking correlate with increased activation of the dopamine reward system.

Recall the primary somatosensory cortex at the front of the parietal lobes where the "skin meets the brain." There is a similar structure adjacent to this at the back of the frontal lobes with a related function. It is called the primary motor cortex, and it controls all voluntary skeletal muscle movements. Every time a skeletal muscle voluntarily moves, the signal for the movement originated in the primary motor cortex, this is where the brain meets the muscles.

In nature, form follows function and resources are precious. The most efficient use of limited resources offers the greatest probability for survival. It makes sense that the nervous system dedicates many sensory and motor nerves to the hands. Exquisite control here enables us to manipulate the environment. Making a knife or a spear can go a long way in protecting and feeding the clan. Similarly, there is value in sensory and motor nerve distribution to the mouth and tongue. Information about the food we eat is crucial. So it makes sense nature places particular emphasis in these areas.

If form follows function, why then does nature allocate so many resources to the face? What advantage to survival is gained by this expensive design choice? The answer speaks directly to what it means to be human. Humans are social creatures. Our nervous systems are built that way. We need social interaction to function properly. The nerves to and from the face allow for facial expressions which enhance communication and facilitate cooperation. These signals ground us in reality as the facial expressions of others validate perceptions of shared experiences. The simple truth is we need face time with others to be mentally healthy.

This brief tour of the nervous system barely scratched the surface of structures and functions making up this vast seat of human consciousness. Each specialized network in the brain expresses a different facet of emergent consciousness through patterns of signal transfer between the structures having the experience. Each facet of emergent consciousness then associates with many other facets of emergent consciousness to form still other expressions of emergent consciousness. The system is astonishingly complex. Whenever making generalizations about structures and their functions we should always keep in mind, there is much more going on than meets the eye. We will continue to explore the nervous system throughout the remainder of this book, but with the scaffolding now set in place, it is time to consider the basic operating systems of consciousness; the motivators of behavior we call reflex, instinct and instinctively motivated drives.

Stetson C1, Fiesta MP, Eagleman DM. (2007) Dec 12;2(12):e1295. PLoS One☐ Does time really slow down during a frightening event?

Edvard I. Moser, Emilio Kropff, and May-Britt Moser (July 2008) Annual Review of Neuroscience Vol. 31: 69-89 Place Cells, Grid Cells, and the Brain's Spatial Representation System

4 MOTIVATION AND BEHAVIOR

Animal life on Earth usually begins with the joining of sperm and egg. The newly formed zygote undergoes a rapid transformation through a process of cellular division and differentiation which is remarkably similar across species. As the newly differentiated cells become the tissues, organs, and systems of the developing organism the emerging heart begins to beat, the cells destined to become skeletal muscle start to twitch and the early nervous system fires to life forming the initial connections setting the stage for higher consciousness to come into being. It is an amazing process.

Each stage of development can be affected by the environment, so learning, broadly defined, takes place even in utero. From its earliest beginnings to the end of life, the nervous system senses and adapts to change. It was once believed the adult nervous system could not change. The poor prognosis following injury suggested a system fixed in place sometime during adolescence. We now know, though the rate of change slows down, the nervous system continues to adapt throughout the entire lifespan.

It is a fundamental axiom that all behavior is motivated and the primary purpose is survival. Since behaviors is an expenditure of limited resources, greater efficiency will increase survival. These ideas can explain and even predict behavior while at the same time revealing a fundamental purpose for consciousness. One answer to the question, "what is the purpose of consciousnesses?" is, consciousness motivates efficient behavior towards advancing survival..

Human consciousness emerges most directly from the dynamic, transitional and relational signal transfer patterns between neurons in the human brain. Whenever these dynamic, transitional, and relational signals cease, all evidence for consciousness also stops. Because of the constant conjunction between dynamic, transitional, and relational signal transfer in the brain and both consciousness and behavior, it makes sense to say these dynamic, transitional, and relational signal transfer patterns induce both consciousness and behavior.

To better understand the complex signal transfer patterns expressing complex expressions of consciousness and behavior we will begin by examining simple signal transfer patterns inducing simple forms of consciousness and behavior.

The dynamic, transitional and relational signal transfer patterns inducing reflex behaviors occurs between anatomical structures operating below the level of the brain. These signal transfers patterns play out in a cascading domino-like cause and affect sequence between the structures involved.

Reflex behavior is a very simple form of consciousness requiring no previous learning or experience to take place. It is developmentally built-in to the system by virtue or the associations between the structures experiencing the signal transfer process

A simple analog for reflex behavior comes from the properties and behaviors of a rubber ball. A rubber ball rolls downhill simply because of its design. If you toss a rubber ball onto the floor, it will bounce in a very predictable way, again, simply because it is the nature of rubber balls to do so. Similarly, reflexive behaviors unfold due to the cause and effect sequence of events between the anatomical structures experiencing the cascading signal transfer sequence.

The knee-jerk action of the patella reflex occurs when a

mallet strikes the patella tendon of the knee. It plays out at the level of the spinal cord. The knee-jerk behavior emerges from the dynamic, transitional and relational cascading sequence of signal transfer between the anatomical structures involved.

As the mallet strikes the patella tendon, the attached quadriceps muscle group gets briefly tugged. This tug causes stretch receptors within the muscle to send out a signal via the sensory nerve to the dorsal ganglia root located in the spinal cord. Here, the sensory neuron carrying the signal acts directly upon the motor neuron leading back to the quadriceps muscle group initiating a muscle contraction. At the same time, the sensory neuron in the dorsal ganglia root also triggers an inhibitory interneuron which sends a signal to the motor nerve of the opposing hamstring muscle group inhibiting contraction. The knee-jerk behavior occurs independent of the signals which are also simultaneously sent up the spinal cord to the brain for further processing. The reaction can even take place for a short time after decapitation.

Most people do not consider reflex to be conscious. There is, however, good reason to believe all behavior is conscious. The signal transfer sequence inducing the patella reflex is similar to the signal transfer events known to produce consciousness in other systems. Taken as a whole, the structures inducing the patella reflex express awareness of the mallet strike to the patella tendon as evidenced by the knee-jerk response. It is true; this awareness is nowhere near the "I think therefore I am" level of awareness sometimes seen in the human brain. Nevertheless, it is "awareness" as evidenced by behavior. The behavioral response to the mallet strike suggests this sequence qualifies as a simple form of consciousness.

The common denominator is dynamic, transitional and

relational signal transfer causing intelligent behavior. Intelligent behavior just is the telltale sign of consciousness. The dynamic, transitional, and relational signal transfer pattern we call the patella reflex is therefore an example of emergent signal transfer induced consciousness.

Understanding consciousness is challenging in part because consciousness is always a moving target. It is a dynamic, transitional and relational process. That is to say, the signal transfer patterns inducing both behavior and consciousness are themselves dynamic, transitional and relational. It is the interactive patterns of dynamic, transitional and relational signal transfer which produce both the behavior and the consciousness.

Some will recoil at the idea that patterns of dynamic, transitional, and relational signal transfer induce consciousness. Convergent evidence for this idea will be presented throughout the remainder of this book. We are coming to terms here with some pretty complex systems. Understanding the nature of any system requires understanding all of the structurally related elements making up the system.

At this point in the discourse, I am simply planting the seed of an idea with the promise of convergent validity to follow. For the moment, I ask you to remain open to the notion that dynamic, transitional, relational signal transfer induces both behavior and consciousness.

Consciousness is an emergent process. There is no way to directly measure emergent processes because emergent processes are dynamic, transitional and relational. To measure consciousness directly would be like trying to measure a house directly. We could describe the perimeter of a house, but that would not be the house. We could list the elements of a house, such as brick, lumber, wiring, and so on but that too would not be the house. We could describe the thousands of the different interrelated elements making up every aspect of the structure, and no description would accurately represent the totality of the house except the house itself. The game is even rougher than that. All structures are different, and all undergo constant change as they uniquely respond to the environment. So it becomes easy to see why there is no simple way to measure complex structures like houses or consciousness.

Because consciousness cannot be measured directly, we can only infer the consciousness of others through their behavior. The most elemental form of behavior is reflex behavior. The next step up in complexity of behavior from reflex is instinct. Instinctive behaviors are more complicated than reflexive behaviors because instinctive behaviors emerge from more complex signal transfer patterns occurring between structures located in both the body and the brain.

Instincts, by definition, occur in response to a specific stimuli and usually appear during a particular phase of an organism's development. They often play a critical role in the organism's development. That is why they exist. Some instinctive reactions, such as the shaking of water from wet fur, occur across a wide range of species while others, like the building of a bridge by ants using only their bodies, are organism specific.

Like reflex behavior, instinctive reactions occur because of the association between the anatomical structures involved. These responses are built in through the normal developmental process. The same rubber ball analogy used to describe reflex behavior can be used to describe instinctive reactions. The increased complexity of instinct is analogous to a rubber ball striking other rubber balls.

Instinctive actions arise out of the signal transfer

patterns between neurons in the brain responsible for perceiving a stimulus and the neurons responsible for the behavioral response to the stimulus. These structures work in concert with the sensory organ system and the musculoskeletal system to induce the instinctive behavior. Because the clusters of neurons and related structures form a network of association, the activation of the sensing units causes a cascading sequence of signal transfer leading directly to the instinctive behavior.

Instinctive behaviors are often simple but some can be quite complex. For example, a newborn kangaroo is little more than a fetus at birth. This offspring of the Large Red Kangaroo emerges after a brief 33-day gestation period. It is blind, hairless, and only a few centimeters long. The hind legs have not developed at all, but the nervous system has already installed the neurological association networks necessary to perform some pretty sophisticated instinctive behaviors.

After emerging from the birth canal, the Joey uses its forelegs to grasp and climb through the mother's thick fur making its way from the birth canal to the mother's pouch. This perilous journey takes three to five minutes. Once in the pouch, it fastens itself onto one of the mother's four teats and begins to feed. It is likely this behavior is guided by a chemical message emanating from the mother's pouch which she recently licked clean. Following a chemical trail is a common theme in nature.

The role of instinct varies by species. As organisms evolve the role of social learning increases and the role of instinct tends to decrease. Mammals are more dependent upon social learning than are birds, reptiles, amphibians, and fish. For example, lions and chimpanzees raised in zoos without the benefit of natural parenting experiences often reject their offspring because they have not learned parenting skills. In contrast, reptiles do not need these experiences to rear their young. For them, instinct alone gets the job done.

Since all behavior is motivated, the question becomes; what is behavior trying to achieve? In nature, the answer is always survival. Self-preservation is the universal hallmark of life. Motivation is first and foremost about survival.

What might seem to be an exception to the survival rule occurs in the altruistic behaviors of insects launching suicide attacks against threats to the colony. Though they sacrifice themselves, the behavior is self-preservation for the colony as a whole.

The ultimate meaning of any survival is the passing on of DNA to the next generation. Since insect DNA can only be passed on by the colony, self-sacrifice becomes the best way to achieve the survival goal. The same holds true for animals who risk injury or death against more powerful predators while defending their young. Survival, either for the individual or the species as a whole is the prime motivator of all behavior.

Motivation is the willingness to allocate resources toward achieving a goal. High motivation is the willingness to allocate many resources while the absence of motivation is the refusal to allocate any resources at all. It stands to reason, then, in a world with fierce competition for limited resources organisms with strong motivational drives will tend to survive in greater numbers than organisms with weaker motivational drives. Each species then gets propagated by ancestors who have demonstrated the greatest will to live. And so it becomes easy to see how survival becomes the prime motivator of all behavior. All organisms alive today are here because in the crucible of nature's fiercely competitive and unforgiving environment their ancestors demonstrated the strongest will to live.

All creatures attempt to fulfill the survival imperative by seeking benefit or avoiding harm, as such, there is always a relational aspect to any behavior. The driving force for behavior in organisms with more developed consciousness is the expected change in pleasure or pain. Pleasure is the signal experienced as nature's way of motivating behavior while pain is the signal nature uses to inhibit action. For healthy organisms, pleasure becomes associated with that which promotes health while pain becomes associated with that which reduces health. Given the universal survival imperative and the pleasure and pain model of motivation, we can now deduce our basic human motivational drives.

Since understanding is relational and everything hinges on everything else for its context-based meaning, there are many ways to conceptualize a system of motivational drives. That one model reflects reality well does not mean other models are wrong. All understanding is relational, and context is essential. With this caveat in mind, one model of instinctively motivated drives which accounts for the vast majority of human behaviors includes a drive for safety and security, a drive for socialization and a drive for sex.

These instinctively motivated drives help us understand the antecedents of behavior. Though the drives are instinctively motivated, if conflicting forces come into play, behavior can be resisted. There is, however, an important distinction between instinctively motivated drives and a mere inclination to act. Instinctively motivated drives are clarion calls for action. Activation of an instinctively motivated drives will therefore almost always result in behavior.

When an instinctively motivated drive is activated, and behavior takes place, the drive becomes temporarily satisfied, and the organism experiences something of a narcotic effect. It just feels good to satisfy instinctively motivated drives. The good feeling results from activation of the dopamine reward system. Like all narcotic effects, it tends to be insatiable and is easily habit-forming. This is how nature instills survival skills.

To illustrate the difference between an instinctively motivated drive and an inclination, I like to tell a fictitious story about receiving a phone call from an old high school friend. He says he was thinking about the good times way back when and wanted to know how I was doing. He goes on to say he has a copy of that favorite music of the era and he would like to invite me over this afternoon for a tasty lunch, music and memories.

Because I am currently motivated to continue working on this book, I don't think his proposal would activate any of my instinctively motivated drives. I would therefore likely respond with something along the lines of, "Wow that sounds great. I am a little busy today, but sometime soon, maybe next week; we should get together and make that happen." I would then get off the phone and do pretty much what I was planning to do all along. Not much motivation for behavior here.

If, on the other hand, I received a call from Miss Universe excitedly telling me how she just won the lottery. She goes on to say she saw me in the supermarket the other day when she bought her lottery ticket. For her, it was love at first sight, so she followed me out to my car and wrote down my license tag. She then hired a private investigator to get my phone number. I am all she has been able to think about, and she can't live another minute without me in her arms. She wants me to drop everything and come to her beachfront home where she is waiting for me naked in the Jacuzzi with a pizza. See the difference, inclination versus instinctively motivated drive?

Instinctively motivated drives are clarion calls for action, they almost always induce behavior. When satisfied, they tend to generate an insatiable narcotic effect which is easily habit-forming. If Miss Universe were to make that call, all three of my instinctively motivated drives; the drive for safety and security, the drive for socialization and the drive for sex would be activated. This reaction would generate a powerful motivation for me to act. I might knock my mother over as I headed for the door!

The drive for safety and security is the preeminent instinctively motivated drive. When we behave in ways we think will increase our safety and security, it just feels good. We are motivated to seek food, clothing, and shelter because doing so promotes our survival and satisfies our drive for safety and security. It makes sense that safety and security are the primary motivational drivers of behavior because they are a direct expression of the universal survival imperative.

Knowing the motivation for behavior, however, does not always allow for easy prediction. The behavior of plants and bacteria are easy to predict because it is easy to see how their actions affect their survival. For a plant, there is no complicated abstract mental representation of the idea of light to be considered. There is simply light or no light. Light equals safety and security. Light is life. Though humans have the same survival imperative, our behaviors are much harder to predict because they result from many more layers of dynamic, transitional, relational signal transfer.

The prediction game is even trickier than that. Throw in our often faulty perceptions and misunderstandings and then add to the mix the constantly changing cultural norms and it's a wonder we ever get predicting behavior right at all. Though the many layers of human consciousness make prediction difficult, it is almost always easy to see how a behavior was driven by an instinctively motivated drive retrospectively.

The safety and security drive is closely related to the socialization drive because humans are social creatures. The human nervous system needs social interaction to be mentally healthy. So it is not surprising people have a strong instinctively motivated drive for socialization. The socialization drive is an extension of the safety and security survival imperative.

Like all instinctively motivated drives, the drive for socialization feels good when satisfied. The example I use to illustrate the power of the socialization drive is an imaginary gathering of my peers who have come together to recognize my achievements. They spontaneously erupt in song, "for he's a jolly good fellow whom nobody can deny." It feels good to be lovingly accepted by others.

The instinctively motivated drive for socialization begins at an early age due to our dependence upon caregivers. When a child is warmly encouraged and applauded the effect can be so powerful it changes physiology. You can practically see them grow right before your eyes. When deprived of this vital support, children often fail to thrive.

Hospitals used to place premature infants in isolettes, so called because they isolate the baby from the environment. Today, neonatal intensive care units encourage interaction like touch therapy because they know even premature infants benefit from social connections.

As with safety and security motivated behaviors, predicting socialization motivated behavior is difficult, but here again, it is often easy to see how a behavior was motivated by the socialization drive retrospectively.

Sex is the third instinctively motivated drive. Like the drives for safety and security and socialization, the instinctively motivated drive for sex is also an expression of the survival imperative. Ultimately it is only through sex that most of us achieve enduring survival. All creatures die. The only possibility for continued existence in corporeal form is through the passing on of DNA, and this usually means sex. Is it any wonder then sex plays such a significant role in society. Few readers will need an example of the power of the sexual instinct to appreciate the forces involved. For any doubters, consider Madison Avenue's multi-billion dollar advertising industry.

Capitalism is all about motivating behavior. Companies play on all of our motivational drives, but the motivational drive they play on most is sex. Advertisers satisfy their capitalistic drive for money by promising to satisfy our instinctively motivated drives for survival. They are not selling cars; they are selling safety and security, socialization and most of all, sex. They wouldn't spend the money if it didn't work. The obvious appeal to our sex instinct is so pervasive that an ad campaign specifically designed to exclude sexual content might succeed simply due to its novelty.

Behaviors expressed in our attempts to satisfy the sex instinct can include pretty much anything under the sun. As a young man, I was led to believe growing my hair long would increase the probability of satisfying my instinctively motivated drive for sex. I grew my hair long. If they told me wearing green lipstick would work, I bet I would have worn green lipstick.

Some young men today wear their pants in, shall we say, an equatorial fashion. This style takes lots of effort to get just right. Constant adjustment and readjustment, too high and you're Urkel, too low and they fall to the ground. There must be some strong motivational forces at work here to justify this significant expenditure of energy and effort.

The ancient Greeks had keen insight into derivative forms of the sex instinct. They called the sex drive Eros. To the Greeks, Eros was not simply the force which produced beautiful eight-pound babies with the world as their oyster. No, Eros is a highly destructive force. Eros is the force behind rape, pillage, and plunder.

When someone drives a car aggressively, they are figuratively mounting the other drivers. This is Eros. And it is Eros which says, "You don't cut me off buddy, I cut you off" as we aggressively react. It is called road rage, and it should be avoided at all costs because instinctively motivated drives tend to block higher level rational thought.

Instinctive drives block rational thought because they emerge from our survival imperative and activation of the autonomic nervous system. This emotional energy comes from the lower level survival based alligator brain which tends to block the more deliberative higher level neocortex.

Although nature created our instinctively motivated drives to promote survival within the environments in which we developed, their activation today in modern society causes people to make bad choices in places like casinos, sales showrooms, political conventions and sports arenas.

In summary, all behavior is motivated. The survival imperative expresses itself through the instinctively motivated drives for safety and security, socialization, and sex. These drivers of behavior act as the base operating system upon which all higher levels of consciousness operate. Understanding their influence allows us to level the playing field between the alligator brain and the higher level neocortex. Now that we appreciate the base motivational operating system of consciousness, we can turn our attention to the way new information gets integrated into a nervous system. Learning how new experience gets integrated into the nervous system will help us understand the relationship between signal transfer and consciousness.

5 ASSOCIATION AND LEARNING

We began by describing the compare and contrast process of categorization. We then looked at the associations of simple organisms. Next we toured the nervous system and then described the motivators of behavior called reflex, instinct, and instinctively motivated drive. To the uninitiated, this may seem somewhat disjointed, but we are creating a path here with plenty of bread crumbs. Ultimately, we are weaving together a tapestry of comprehension out of which will emerge understanding of the nature of consciousness. The next thread in our fabric of knowledge is to explore how new information gets integrated into a nervous system. Understanding how new information is added will help us appreciate the way all information is processed.

Aristotle said, "All men by nature desire to know. An indication of this is the delight we take in our senses; for even apart from their usefulness they are loved for themselves and above all others the sense of sight. For not only with a view to action, but even when we are not going to do anything, we prefer sight to almost everything else. The reason is that this, most of all the senses, makes us know and brings to light many differences between things." Here Aristotle equates learning with awareness of the "many differences between things." Understanding how the nervous system "brings to light many differences between things" for us begins with a definition of learning.

Learning is defined as the relatively permanent change in behavior brought about through experience. Many are surprised to discover learning hinges on behavior rather than thought. It does so because the evidence for learning is almost always behavioral.

Sometimes the evidence something has been learned is the learner saying they have learned something. "Saying" is a behavior. Someday brain imaging techniques will allow us to witness on a molecular level the process of learning within the brain, even then I suspect behavior will remain the variable of choice because it is with behavior, as they say, "the rubber meets the road."

Not all changes in behavior result from learning. There are developmental changes across the lifespan which are not the result of experience per se. Many of these changes occur slowly, often imperceptibly over time. Then there are also changes which result from insult or injury to the system. So changes in behavior reflecting shifts in the nervous system can occur through natural development, injury and the process we call learning.

All healthy nervous systems change. Change distinguishes between a healthy nervous system and coma. Change is life. Life is change. Trying to maintain any state of consciousness, even a desirable one, is actually equivalent to a death wish. Since change is coming, the question becomes how best to increase the probability of healthy change? This next sentence expresses a very important idea. Understanding the way information is coded into the nervous system can help you make the changes most likely to result in a flourishing life.

The key to learning is "association." By association, I mean connection. If you didn't know association means connection, that just means the clusters of neurons in the language processing area of your brain did not have a functional association or connection between the group of neurons activated when you think "association" and the cluster of neurons activated when you think "connection." Now that you do know association means connection, these two groups of neurons have a stronger association or connection between themselves. Activating one cluster now tends to stimulate the other. When this happens, as far as the brain is concerned, this equals that within the given context, association equals connection.

Learning just is the creation or altering of connections between neurons in the brain. There are several ways these connections can be altered or created. In order of increasing complexity, they are habituation and sensitization, classical conditioning, operant conditioning, and modeling. As the complexity of learning advances the level of information abstraction also increases.

The simplest form of learning is habituation and sensitization. Habituation and sensitization are called non-associative learning because the connections being altered are already present before the new learning takes place. Habituation and sensitization alter existing connections between neurons.

Remember, with learning; we are talking about connections between clusters of neurons which perform different functions. For example, there is a group of neurons in my brain which becomes activated when I perceive my daughter's face. The act of recognizing her face for me just is the cascading signal transfer pattern of this particular cluster of neurons. That is just what happens in my brain when I perceive my daughter's face.

Now, this group of neurons is associated with many other groups of neurons each of which performs a different cognitive function. I like my daughter. This means the cluster of neurons activated when I perceive her face is already strongly associated with the neurons in the reward centers of my brain. Because of this association, when I recognize my daughter's face I tend to feel good. This neural association began a long time ago and has been reinforced many times since. The strength of associations gets adjusted through the fine-tuning process we call habituation and sensitization.

Habituation and sensitization are nature's way of changing the amplitude or intensity of an established stimulus and response pair. A stimulus is anything sensed or perceived, and a response is any reaction to the sensation or perception. The strength of these associations can increase or decrease sort of like a dimmer switch for a variable intensity light.

Whenever a stimulus is deemed to be neither rewarding nor harmful, the learner tends to habituate. The stimulus then becomes relatively unimportant. The nervous system will instead focus on more salient information signals. Habituation reduces the intensity of the stimulus and response circuit.

Going the other way, with sensitization the reaction to a stimulus is amplified following successive exposures. In this case, the stimulus is seen as increasingly rewarding or harmful as the case may be. The increasing annoyance from a dripping faucet or a nagging child occurs due to sensitization increasing the intensity of the stimulus and response circuit.

Habituation and sensitization are continually fine-tuning the nervous system. Stimulus, sensation, perception and response are best understood as a relational process and explicitly not static events. They represent change in a system that never stops changing. Knowing how the systems works allows us to make better choices.

Case in point, I recently had lunch with a friend at a restaurant. After the main course, we decided to take the experience to the next level by sharing a piece of pineapple upside down cheesecake. Because I happen to be writing this book, I was keenly aware of habituation and sensitization. I knew the initial bite of the cake would be, for me, as good as it gets because my nervous system would quickly habituate to the cake stimulus. For me, the experience would soon turn into a chase after the initial sensation of pleasure with inevitable diminishing returns. That is just how the reward system operates.

So I cleansed my palate with a sip of water and prepared myself with maximum awareness for the impending culinary delight. I took the first bite and allowed myself to feel the entire experience. Two more fully conscious bites and I knew the delightful part of the experience was over for me. We left the remainder of the cake on the table and avoided much of the discomfort we would have experienced from a sugar rush and crash.

Habituation and sensitization occur in every species studied including the single-celled protozoa Stentor Coeruleus (Wood, 1969). The habituation and sensitization of protozoa is an early expression of the "will" for more or less of a stimulus. In more complex creatures, this will is reflected in the expected change in the level of pleasure or pain calling for more or less of an experience.

The motivational dance between pleasure and pain is complicated. During my recent lunch date I was able to experience the pleasure of cheesecake, but not without some degree of pain instigated by clusters of neurons clamoring for more. This instinctively programmed response to sweet, fatty foods was critically important for our ancestors back when these energy rich foods were hard to find during early in human development. Today, this instinctively motivated safety and security drive combined with an abundance of easily obtained calories are the primary cause of obesity, heart disease, high blood pressure and type-two diabetes. Knowing how the system operates can help us maximize healthy pleasures while minimizing pain and illness.

Before we look at how new associations are formed, now is a good time to review the relationship between signal transfer patterns between neurons and consciousness. It is clusters of nerve cells working in concert with other groups of nerves cells which together induce the shifting fabric of human consciousness. If I were to ask, for instance, "what color was your first bicycle?" most people easily recall this kind of information. Leaving aside the many signal processing events that happen before a desire to remember the information, the retrieval of information itself goes something like this.

Individual neurons alone have very little information processing power. They are, after all, just tiny biological on and off switches which flash on only briefly when triggered. Like the pixels on a video screen, each pixel can not convey much information. It is only in association with many other pixels that an image emerges. Similarly, information gets encoded in the brain by clusters of neurons associated with many other clusters of neurons.

Each nerve cell within a cluster associates with the other nerve cells of that cluster. They have formed synaptic pathways of communication with one another. That's what makes them a cluster! As each group of neurons is activated, it resonates with a particular awareness in the same way the activation of a specific pattern of pixels on a television screen resonates with a particular image. It is the dynamic, transitional and relational signal transfer patterns of changing neural activations which we experience as unfolding consciousness.

Earlier we described the relationship between consciousness and intelligent behavior as being the result of cascading signal transfer patterns between associated structures. We then considered the patella reflex to be a simple example of intelligent behavior emerging from a simple cascading signal transfer pattern suggesting something like elemental consciousness. The concert of associations between the stretch receptor, sensory nerve, motor nerve, inhibitory interneuron and muscle fibers together functioned as an "emergent awareness" of the mallet striking the tendon, and so together these structures exhibit properties similar to the clusters of neurons in the brain generally recognized to induce consciousness. It is true the patella reflex is not a high-resolution array of awareness like those sometimes seen in the brain, but I hope the reader can now begin to appreciate the way consciousness emerges from dynamic, transitional and relational signal transfer patterns between networked structures.

We have insight into the nature of memory storage and retrieval from observations made during brain surgery. Brain tissue has no pain receptors because there is no evolutionary advantage to having pain receptors in the brain tissue itself. Once the saber tooth tiger has your skull open, it is pretty much game over. There are pain receptors in the brain lining and blood vessels, and these receptors are usually the cause headaches.

Since there are no pain receptors in the brain tissue, patients can be kept awake during brain surgery to assist by answering questions. Areas of the brain being considered for incision are stimulated with a probe before cutting to assure vital neurological functions are not damaged. If the patient indicates a stimulated area is important "hey, that's my piano lessons," the surgeon will consider a different site for incision.

Patients stimulated in this way sometimes report experiencing vivid memories of long ago events. These memories contain detailed sensory information including sight, sound, smell, taste and tactile sensations all experienced as if the event were occurring in the present moment. Clusters of neurons working together with other groups of neurons have stored these memories. We know the brain stores these memories in many different groups of neurons because of the different areas of the brain involved including sight, sound, smell, taste, and touch.

Most neurons stimulated in this way do not produce these dramatic effects. The absence of effect is not surprising when we consider the storage capacity of 100 billion neurons. That's a lot of potential clusters. Additionally, because each neuron can associate with several different clusters, the permutations for information storage are greater than 100 billion neurons would otherwise suggest. The brain makes new connections all the time and old connections can be blocked or abandoned when obsolete.

So knowing is expressed by the signal transfer patterns between clusters of neurons and learning is the formation of new associations between existing groups of neurons. When learning occurs, the newly combined neural structure expresses a new signal transfer pattern representing the new awareness of the newly learned information.

Increasing the number of stimulus and response circuits within a nervous system increases an organism's situational awareness as evidenced by an increase in the number of potential responses to a given stimulus challenge. The ability to learn from new experience by creating new associations between stimulus and response circuits representing new behaviors is how consciousness advances.

With just a few nerves networked together, simple organisms can regulate some highly complex behaviors. The roundworm Caenorhabditis Elegans (C. Elegans), with only 302 nerve cells, exhibits a complex sensory awareness of the environment with a sophisticated set of motor responses all facilitated through an integrated spinal cord-like neural pathway. The worm's primitive nervous system utilizes neurotransmitters for communication between neurons much like our own and the worm demonstrates a capacity for memory and learning. Caenorhabditis Elegans, with just 13,000 genes, can "learn" through classical conditioning to avoid a previously attractive stimulus (Morrison, Wen, Runciman, van der Kooy, 1999).

For C. Elegans to learn something new means the worm's nervous system has created a new association or connection between the structures responsible for sensing a stimulus and the structures responsible for the new behavior. To be attracted to a stimulus means there is already a neurological association between the structures responsible for sensing the attractive stimulus and the structures responsible for moving towards the stimulus. Before the new learning took place, this connection already existed. As far as the worm was concerned, sensing the attractive stimulus equaled moving towards the stimulus.

Learning to avoid a previously attractive stimulus is best explained by the formation of a new association between the stimulus sensing structures and what amounts to the worm's pain awareness structures. Once this new connection is formed, as far as the worm is concerned, previously attractive stimulus now equals "pain response" and so the worm moves away. Classical conditioning is a bona fide form of associative learning, and for a creature with just 302 nerves cells, it is quite an accomplishment.

In the compare and contrast model of knowing, whenever a cluster of neurons becomes associated with another group of neurons, in at least one context (cluster of clusters), they are grouped into the same category of understanding. When this happens, as far as the brain is concerned, "this" then equals "that." We will now explore the three types of associative learning called classical conditioning, operant conditioning and modeling.

Our understanding of classical conditioning began with the work of Ivan Pavlov when he noticed the dogs in his lab began to salivate before the presentation of food. We do not know what caused this salivation response, but anyone with a dog might guess.

It could have been the sound of the dog food bag opening. It might have been the appearance of the lab assistant who routinely fed the animals. Whatever the cause, Pavlov realized an association had been formed which caused salivation before the presentation of food and so he decided to study the process.

He set up formal experiments designed to create a new association between the sound of a bell and salivation. The classical conditioning trials he conducted went something like this. Ring the bell, present the food and observe salivation. Then again: Bell, food, salivation. He repeated the closely timed sequence until a new neurological association was formed. At this point, the series was changed to Bell, no food, salivation. Voila, one classically conditioned K-9! The dog had been classically conditioned to associate the sound of a bell with food. As far as the dog's salivation response was concerned, "Bell" now equals "food." Pavlov published his results and won a Nobel Prize.

Before the conditioning trials, the dog already had a cluster of neurons which caused salivation. The dog also had a group of neurons which became active whenever the dog perceived food. These two groups of neurons were already strongly associated with each other. They were part of the same stimulus and response network. Activate the food perception cluster, and the salivation cluster became active. We know they were part of the same system because the dog salivated in response to food.

The sound of the bell activated a completely different cluster of neurons. Initially, the bell perception neurons had no association with either the food perception cluster or the salivation response cluster. The repeated pairing of Bell and food stimulus forged a new connection between the bell perception neurons and the food perception neurons. At that point, as far as the dog's brain was concerned, Bell equals food. Bell and food were both placed in the same category of "things to salivate about." The neurons had forged new synaptic connections. With the new association, we see a new pattern of dynamic, transitional and relational signal transfer which now induces a new emergent consciousness expressed as the new behavior.

Classical conditioning is responsible for many of our reflexive responses such as phobia, disgust, nausea, anger, fear and sexual arousal. It helps us understand some otherwise puzzling aspects of human behavior. For example, sexual fetishes probably have their origins in classically conditioned experiences.

To summarize, classical conditioning occurs when a previously neutral stimulus is repeatedly presented together with a reflex eliciting stimulus until the neutral stimulus elicits the conditioned response. Classical conditioning is the creation of a new association between a stimulus and reflexive response.

Like classical conditioning, operant conditioning is the formation of a new association between neurons. The difference between classical conditioning and operant conditioning is the type of neurons associated. Classical conditioning deals with the associations between clusters of neurons which perceive a stimulus and neurons which initiate a reflex response. Operant conditioning is the formation of a new association between the neurons responsible for voluntary behavior and neurons responsible for evaluating the outcome of the behavior. Classical conditioning modifies reflex while operant conditioning modifies voluntary behavior.

Operant conditioning hinges on the consequences of a behavior. The outcomes of behavior can be pleasure or pain. Generally speaking, pleasure is nature's way of getting us to do things while pain is nature's way of getting us to stop doing things.

In the language of operant conditioning, "positive" means pleasure or pain increases while "negative" means pleasure or pain decreases. Because perceptions of both pleasure and pain can either increase or decrease this leads to four potential outcomes for behavior, more pleasure, less pleasure, more pain and less pain.

Positive reinforcement occurs when the behavior outcome increases pleasure; like getting a cookie. Negative reinforcement occurs when the outcome decreases pain; such as leaving a noisy environment. Repeating a behavior is more likely with both positive and negative reinforcement.

Positive punishment, usually just called punishment, occurs when pain follows an action, such as a spanking. Negative punishment occurs when pleasure is reduced following a behavior, such as taking away a toy. Both positive and negative punishments reduce the probability a behavior will be repeated.

It is also possible for an action to result in no change in pain or pleasure. Since all behavior is motivated, actions with no change in pain or pleasure will tend to habituate and go away on their own. All this may sound rather bland and academic, but the utility for behavioral change is indisputable. If you want to learn or teach new tricks, these principles properly applied will do the job nicely.

When my daughter was about two years old, I took a class on infant and childhood development. I remember the day I learned the essence of these principles. The class was discussing spanking. I shared my belief at the time that spanking a child to discourage dangerous behavior, such as running out into the street, is a good idea. I believed spanking would help the child remember. In my mind, spanking was not only justified, failing to spank might be negligent.

That day my professor was Dr. Mary Levitt. Dr. Levitt responded to my idea with a slightly pained expression on her face as she lovingly said to me in front of the class; "It is true we spank our children, but when we spank our children what we are teaching them is, if you don't get what you want, hit. Because you didn't get what you wanted and you hit." I was both surprised and impressed. The more I thought about it, the more I became convinced she was right. If you want to extinguish a behavior, the evidence suggests the best way to do so is to ignore the behavior while reinforcing other more desirable behaviors.

Let's look at what is going on in the brain during operant conditioning. Once again, association is the name of the game. Operant conditioning is the formation of a new association between some cluster of neurons responsible for a voluntary behavior and some other group of neurons responsible for assessing the outcome of the action. Since classical conditioned modifies reflex behavior and operant conditioning modifies voluntary behavior, to appreciate the difference between classical conditioning and operant conditioning, we need to understand the difference between a reflex and a voluntary behavior.

Reflex actions occur in the absence of voluntary control. They tend to originate in the more primal areas of the nervous system. All voluntary muscle movements, on the other hand, arise in that strip of the brain located at the rear of the frontal lobes called the primary motor cortex. Because operant conditioning is an association between a voluntary behavior and the behavioral outcome, these new associations are between clusters of neurons in the higher level association cortex. The fundamental difference between classical and operant conditioning is, classical conditioning modifies lower level reflex behaviors while operant conditioning modifies higher level voluntary actions.

Now let's consider what is going on when we find something rewarding. The frontal lobes contain most of the dopamine-sensitive neurons in the brain. This dopamine neurotransmitter system facilitates reward, attention, short-term memory, planning, motivation, and arousal. It plays a significant role in all reward-motivated behaviors studied. When you find something rewarding, chances are your brain just got a hit of dopamine.

Parkinson's disease results from an insufficient action of dopamine in the brain. A study of patients with Parkinson's disease (Frank et al., 2004) showed that while the patients were off their dopamine-enhancing medication, they tended to learn more readily from adverse consequences than from positive reinforcement. In the absence of the drug which increased the effect of dopamine, positive reinforcement was less effective. Conversely, when taking their medications patients showed the opposite tendency. Overall, positive reinforcement was found to be a more effective than punishment. This supports the idea that learning from positive reinforcement is associated with the dopamine reward system.

The assessment of pain can occur through several channels, but when something is extremely painful, the fight or flight response becomes active. This reaction originates in the lower level alligator brain. While the reward centers use dopamine, the reptilian brain uses the neurotransmitter acetylcholine. Acetylcholine stimulates the secretion of the adrenal corticotrophic hormone (ACTH) which in turn stimulates the adrenal glands to release adrenalin as part of the fight or flight response. When you find something extremely threatening, chances are your system just got a dose of acetylcholine.

Perceptions of reward and punishment are of course much more complicated than the simple expression of dopamine and acetylcholine. Dopamine and acetylcholine work in other systems performing other functions and other neurotransmitters influence perceptions of reward and punishment. Perception is a complex process.

Fight or flight activation has been shown to inhibit the reward circuits supporting the idea that pain and pleasure are in some ways a continuum. These two neural pathways overlap explaining why fear and pain can block pleasure. It is sometimes said "you can catch more flies with honey than vinegar" and this is certainly true for operant conditioning because of the systems involved.

Whenever the fight or flight system is engaged, higher level neurological processing tends to go off-line. These areas are therefore less available for new learning. Autonomic activation is why spanking is not as useful as positively reinforcing more desired behaviors. Alligators are hard to domesticate.

So the associations of operant conditioning are between clusters of neurons responsible for perceptions of pleasure or pain and groups of neurons responsible for generating the behavior. Groups of neurons representing awareness of behavioral outcomes tend to be more abstract than the stimulus and response circuits of reflex action. These outcome evaluations are assessed in the association cortex as the organism imagines the experience. Because these outcomes are imagined, they tend to be subjective and abstract.

When something is considered concrete, this is just another way of saying the associations involved are rigidly categorized. As far as the brain is concerned, this just equals that. When something is considered abstract, the neural connections interact with several potential clusters of awareness representing several different contexts for understanding.

Behavior tends to be concrete but the perceptions of behaviors and behavioral outcomes tends to be abstract. Since both the cognitive representations of a behavior and behavioral outcomes of operant conditioning are more subjective than the concrete stimulus and response of classical conditioning, operant conditioning is more abstract than classical conditioning.

In summary, operant conditioning is the formation of new associations between clusters of neurons responsible for voluntary behavior and neurons responsible for the mental representation of the behavioral outcome. The third type of associative learning we will explore is called modeling.

Modeling is learning through observation; it is a "monkey see, monkey do," kind of process. There are two types of modeling. The first is called imprinting and the second is usually just called modeling.

Imprinting is the phase-dependent observational learning characterized by a rapid onset independent of behavioral outcome. We see the effects of imprinting in birds raised in captivity. Birds raised by humans will tend to mark or imprint the human caregiver as the parent and so will often fail to parent their own offspring. To avoid this, when raising California condor chicks for release into the wild, caregivers use a condor hand puppet during feeding.

Imprinting may also occur in humans. The Westermarck effect is thought to be a type of reverse sexual partner imprinting in humans raised together from birth to about six years of age. The usual pattern marks siblings, parents, and other household members as non-sexual or mating partners.

Joseph Shepher (1971) examined the marriage patterns of children raised on communal farms. Out of the nearly 3,000 marriages considered, only fourteen were between children from the same peer group, and none of these were reared together during the first six years of life.

The more well-known type of observational learning is usually just called modeling. It is based on Albert Bandura's Social Learning Theory. It differs from imprinting by being outcome dependent and is not related to any particular phase of development.

Modeling is learning through observation. Both operant conditioning and modeling involve the formation of new associations between a behavior and behavioral outcome. With modeling, the behavior and the outcome are experienced vicariously through observation or imagination of others.

A social model is usually someone of higher authority or status. This type of learning occurs without the learner's "conscious" awareness. It results from witnessing behavior and can sometimes take years to emerge. I have been surprised by behaviors modeled by my parents spontaneously emerging from me while parenting my own child. These actions tend to be related to discipline and dominance. It seems we reach back into childhood as we try to figure out how to be a parent.

Modeling allows behaviors to quickly spread across a

culture through a process called a diffusion chain. Not long ago almost all movie stars modeled smoking and drinking behavior. The culture then adopted these modeled behaviors. When screen practices were adjusted to better align with public health concerns, there was a dramatic drop in these harmful behaviors. There is good reason advertisers regularly spend about 300 billion dollars per year in the United States (roughly 2% of GDP) trying to influence our behaviors through modeling. They do so because it works.

In modeling, new neurological associations occur between clusters of neurons which imagine a behavior and groups of neurons which imagine the behavior's outcome. These new neural connections increase or decrease the probability a behavior will be repeated in the same way as operant conditioning. The fundamental difference between operant conditioning and modeling is who performs the action. With operant conditioning, the responses are carried out by the learner, with modeling the actions are done by others real or imagined.

Let's take a look at what is happening in the brain across all the three modalities of associative learning. By this time, it should be as plain as the nose on your face that association is the name of the game. All new learning is the formation of new neural associations. Classical conditioning is the formation of an association between clusters of neurons responsible for awareness of a stimulus and groups of neurons responsible for a reflexive behavior. Operant conditioning is the formation of an association between groups of neurons responsible for a voluntary behavior and clusters of neurons which assess the outcome of the action. And modeling is the formation of a new association between groups of neurons responsible for observing or imagining a behavior and clusters of neurons which assess the likely outcome of the behavior.

The creation of new connections occurs throughout, what changes is the level of abstraction in the cognitive representations of reality. In classical conditioning, there is essentially no abstract representation of reality. Both the stimulus and reflex response tend to be concrete. This learning occurs below the level of self-aware processing. In operant conditioning, concrete behaviors are associated with more abstract perceptions of an outcome, and in modeling we see the entire process playing out abstractly in the mind of the learner.

It is no coincidence that as the complexity of learning increases; we see a shift in the language commonly used to describe it. Initially, we speak in concrete objective terms like stimulus and response. As we progress towards the increasing complexity of abstract learning, we begin to talk of consciousness and thought. This is an important distinction; because it is here, we start to come to terms with this thing we call "the mental."

Now that we see how learning emerges from new neurological associations between clusters of neurons, in the next chapter, we will consider how temporarily blocking neurological associations creates the spotlight of our conscious attention. Association and learning in conjunction with dissociation and attention are the bricks and mortar of conscious experience.

Michael J. Frank, Lauren C. Seeberger, and Randall C. O'Reilly (2004) "By Carrot or by Stick: Cognitive Reinforcement Learning in Parkinsonism," Science 4, November 2004

Morrison GE, Wen JY, Runciman S, van der Kooy D.

(1999) Olfactory associative learning in Caenorhabditis Elegans. Behavioral Neuroscience. 113: 358-67. PMID 10357460 DOI: 10.1037/0735-7044.113.2.358

Shepher, Joseph. (1971). "Mate Selection Among Second-Generation Kibbutz Adolescents☐ and Adults: Incest Avoidance and Negative Imprinting." Archives of Sexual Behavior 1:293–307.

Wood, David C. (1969). "Electrophysiological studies of the protozoan, Stentor Coeruleus." Journal of Neurobiology 1(4): 363-377. <http://hdl.handle.net/2027.42/50072>

6 DISSOCIATION AND ATTENTION

Creating a new association between neurons allows for the simple learning of the worm C. Elegans described in the last chapter. As nervous systems advance in complexity, the number of potential responses for a given stimulus increases. This can create a competition for action between the stimulus and response circuits calling for different behaviors in response to the same stimulus. In simple nervous systems, these conflicts get resolved by the relative strength of the stimulus response network. As nervous systems become more complex calls for conflicting behaviors will reduce efficiency of the organism as it struggles to choose the best response.

If there is no urgency, the organism can afford to take the extra time necessary for trial and error to work out a good solution. When time is of the essence and life hangs in the balance blocking associations can save time and increase survival. This blocking action is the neurological dissociation function.

It is not clear where in nature neurological dissociation first appears. Our best hope for finding the origins of dissociation comes with the application of two scientific principles. The first principle is "form follows function," and in nature, the primary function is always survival. The second principle is called "Occam's razor." This is the principle of parsimony, economy, and succinctness. Occam's razor states: with competing theories, the simplest, that is, the one with the fewest assumptions is usually correct. Occam's razor cuts away the superfluous.

Using these two principles, we can deduce dissociation will come into play when it offers a significant survival advantage. The simplest forms of consciousness don't need dissociation to get the job done. For simple creatures, stimulus and response circuits are either called for, or they are not. It is only with more complex systems with competing association networks that dissociation offers a significant advantage. Here, selecting the "right" behavior at the right time can mean the difference between life and death.

We see a form of dissociation in some species of fish. Fish predate amphibians and reptiles. Nimbochromis is a fish endemic to Lake Malawi in East Africa. They are called Sleeper Cichlids because of their unusual hunting behavior. These large predatory fish lie on their side at the bottom of the lake and assume a blotchy coloration. Scavengers attracted to what looks like a free meal who venture too close pay the ultimate price.

Now, what could be more stimulating to a hungry Sleeper Cichlid than the presentation of food? The nervous system of this creature must be actively inhibiting the impulse to strike until the time is just right. In spite of a high motivation to act, dissociation blocks the impulse, for a time, thereby increasing the probability Nimbochromis will survive.

As the complexity of nervous systems grows and creatures shift from being reactors to the environment to actors upon the environment, there is more for the organism to "think" about. Before this stage in development, most people would not even use the word think in describing the stimulus and response behaviors of simple creatures. There is, after all, no apparent volitional aspect to reflex responses and so no evidence for what most people would call consciousness.

With the development of dissociation and the capacity to select several potential responses, we see the emergence of a consciousness seemingly exhibiting a "will" as evidenced by the Sleeper Cichlid waiting to strike until the time is just right. In effect, however crudely, the Sleeper Cichlid has cognitively modeled reality to better predict hunting success. It just is the primary function of consciousness to model reality to predict outcomes for increasing survival.

As stated earlier, the word most often used as a synonym for the word consciousness is the word awareness. To be conscious is to be aware, and to be aware is to be aware of something. That is about as far as most people get when they try to focus their conscious awareness on what it means to have conscious awareness.

Most people experience their own conscious awareness without much conscious awareness of their conscious awareness. I have learned the easiest way to get someone to focus their conscious awareness on their conscious awareness is to accuse them of being without conscious awareness.

To become aware of something requires the focus of attention. Attention is a relational process. Focusing attention on one aspect of consciousness requires the relative dissociation of concentration from all other areas of potential awareness, so the focusing of attention compartmentalizes experience. Said another way, the signal transfer pattern between neurons inducing one particular conscious experience is a relative dissociation from all other signal patterns of neurons producing other consciousness experiences.

We defined "knowing" as the categorization of ideas based on the process of compare and contrast. One reason we have difficulty understanding the category we call "consciousness" is we have no experience with awareness other than "consciousness." If you are aware of something, by definition that perception falls into the category "conscious."

It is likely fish have no awareness of water for the same reason. That is, fish typically do not experience categories other than water. Like fish unaware of water, we have difficulty understanding consciousness because, for us, consciousness is the water in which we swim.

So just what is consciousness? Once we begin to ask in earnest, we seem to find more questions than answers. Are you conscious? Were you conscious before I asked? Are you conscious while sleeping? What about dreaming? Are dreams a form of consciousness? Is there subconscious-awareness? How could we know there is a subconscious awareness if it exists apart from waking consciousness? When did my consciousness come into being? Was I conscious before my birth? Will I be conscious after my death?

How about puppies? Are animals conscious? Do puppies have a subconscious mind? Insects have awareness of their surroundings. They respond to the environment and communicate with each other via pheromones and behaviors. Are ants and bees conscious? Sometimes colonies of insects behave like a single organism. Could this be a form of group consciousness? How about plants? They grow towards the light. This requires awareness. Are plants conscious? If plants are conscious, what about rocks, can inanimate objects be aware too? Do computers have consciousness? How about the nonmaterial; do ideas themselves have a consciousness?

There are differences between the various "states" of human consciousness. Using the word "state" to describe consciousness tends to obscure its true nature because consciousness can never actually be a state. The word state suggests a static condition and consciousness is always dynamic, transitional and relational. For ease of communication, I will sometimes refer to specific patterns of signal transfer induced consciousness as being a state all the while keeping in mind that consciousness is, and must always be dynamic, transitional and relational. By comparing and contrasting the different states of consciousness, we will learn more about consciousness itself. One altered state is called sleep. Let's start there.

It is indeed a curious phenomenon that we so casually surrender ourselves over to the "unconscious" state of sleep. During sleep, we experience altered consciousness. Dreams, for instance, can seem magical and bizarre with perceptions of a somehow alternate dream reality. In most cases, it is only after waking that we become aware a dream was only a dream. So, with some states of consciousness, we see a blurring between the categories "real" and "fantasy." The blurring of reality has a mystical feel to it. Is it any wonder then, when speaking of consciousness we use words like "spirit" or "soul?" We are, after all, exploring the very essence of who we think we are.

Let's turn to the natural world for better understanding of sleep. The nematode worm is one of the most primitive organisms to engage in something like sleep. Some fish also appear to sleep. All reptiles, all birds, and all mammals sleep. It seems once a certain level of neurological sophistication emerges sleep becomes essential.

Now there are dangers associated with this altered state of consciousness characterized by reduced awareness of the environment. On the face of it, sleeping seems to conflict with the universal survival imperative. There must be some important advantage to sleeping or nature would not select it. To compensate for a reduced awareness of the environment during sleep nature has engineered some ingenious adaptations.

Sea mammals are especially prone to the dangers of

sleep. They need to regularly surface in order to breathe and must be continually on guard against predators. The human way of sleeping is far too risky for these vulnerable creatures. So whales and dolphins engage in unihemispheric sleep. That's right, only half of their brain sleeps at a time. In this way, they can continue to breathe and stay on guard while still getting the sleep their brains need.

Seals also sleep in this way while out at sea, but revert to a bihemispheric sleep when on land (Oleg I. 2008). None of my students were able to guess at this adaptation and I doubt I would have either. I suspect this is due to false assumptions about consciousness. Most people wrongly believe they are of one mind.

Humans experience five different stages of sleep each distinguished by different brain wave patterns. Brain waves are the measured effect of the electrochemical activity of neurons in the brain. We measure brain waves with electrodes on the scalp which assess the direction, strength, and location of neural activity in the brain. Brain wave activity can range from flat line to frantic storm-like seizures. Different patterns of brain waves are associated with the different stages of sleep and with the various states of waking consciousness.

One brain wave pattern of particular interest to researchers is called Rapid Eye Movement (REM). REM sleep is also known as an "autonomic storm" of brain wave activity so called because the fight or flight system is active during this stage of sleep. REM corresponds with our most vivid and intense dreams. Now it would be dangerous to flail around on the ground while REM dreaming alerting predators to an easy kill, so nature induces paralysis during REM sleep. If you have ever woken up from an intense dream and briefly felt unable to move, this is because you were in fact briefly unable to move.

The dreams of REM sleep have a fight or flight like quality and play out in real time. In contrast, non-REM dreams are less intense and play out in compressed time. Subjects awakened from REM dreams perform differently on tests of emotional affect when compared to subjects awakened from non-REM dreams. Those who just experienced REM dreams showed greater negative affect than those having just experienced non-REM dreams (McNamara et al., 2010). This aligns nicely with what we know about the primal autonomic anger, fear, and lust nervous system. It makes sense that autonomic activation leads to greater negative affect.

REM sleep appears to be essential for proper cognitive function. It seems to be especially important for the consolidation of new procedural and spatial memory. Keep in mind that each new experience is processed by many areas of the brain at nearly the same time. This is a lot of data. It may be that different parts of the brain need to come into some sort of agreement with one another as to the meaning and utility of new experiences.

The perceptual data stream associated with each and every moment of consciousness includes processing from the visual occipital lobes, auditory temporal lobes, tactile parietal lobes, cognitive frontal lobes as well as the more primal gustatory, olfactory, and limbic systems from below the neocortex. The system may need to be taken off-line during sleep to construct a meaningful, unified perceptual awareness of new experiences. New associations must be created cementing in what is useful while discarding the superfluous. It may be sleeping functions as a sort of de-fragmentation of the experiential hard drive. Whatever the purpose, it is evident we experience impaired performance when sleep deprived and extreme deprivation can lead to mental illness up to and including psychosis.

Understanding disorders of sleep allows us to better understand sleep itself. Narcolepsy is a chronic neurological disorder characterized by the brain's failure to normally regulate sleep-wake cycles. During a narcoleptic attack, usually triggered by intense emotional stress with autonomic activation, the narcoleptic experiences a sudden dramatic muscular weakness called cataplexy, their muscles go limp, and they collapse and fall sound asleep.

This reaction to stress is particularly counter-intuitive. Just when things are getting exciting, boom, lights out. What survival advantage could this offer? What is nature up to here?

Narcolepsy may be an atavism. An atavism is an evolutionary throwback. The thinking goes like this; DNA is the molecule in the nucleus of every cell which encodes the instructions for building and replicating the entire organism. It codes for everything from hair color to the number of toes. Similar creatures have similar DNA. There is a direct relationship between the complexity of an organism and complexity of its DNA. When obsolete functions are designed out of the system the genetic code for the function often remains in the DNA in a dormant form which can sometimes be reactivated and expressed.

There is a well-known defense mechanism in nature called the tonic immobility reflex. It is sometimes called "playing possum." It functions as the last line of defense against an attacking predator. The behavior is expressed as complete immobilization in response to extreme activation of the autonomic nervous system. Possum, sheep, goat, mice and many other animals exhibit the tonic immobility reflex. The behavior is adaptive because some predators will not eat an animal which already appears to be dead.

They associate food with live prey. Dead prey may be diseased. Live prey tends to be healthier and safer to eat. Also, actively fighting back will tend to stimulate the attacker's autonomic nervous system thereby increasing the attack behavior. A passive response is less likely to provoke violence.

It makes sense that narcolepsy is an evolutionary atavism. That humans regularly experience paralysis during REM sleep demonstrates the system's current capacity for tonic immobility. Both REM sleep and narcolepsy present with tonic immobility in association with autonomic activation. Looking a little further, we find research suggesting there may be some additional benefit to the tonic immobility response.

Robert Stickgold (2005) conducted studies at Harvard University wherein subjects performed a physically challenging, arcade-style, downhill skiing simulation task. Researchers then monitored the subjects for dream content throughout the night. Those who dreamt about skiing showed significantly better performance when repeating the exercise than those who did not dream about skiing.

We know the brain is always "on the air," always working and ever-changing. It would certainly be advantageous during a period of tonic immobility in response to a threat to run a few cognitive simulations trying to determine the best way to get away safely. The tonic immobility reflex may be a strategy of buying a little time to explore behavioral options. Anecdotal support for this comes from reports of finding a solution to a problem after "sleeping on it." Awakening with a new solution suggests the brain was running simulations during sleep.

The nature of dream consciousness is very different from waking consciousness. If, for instance, while writing these words I was to rise out of my chair and fly into the kitchen for a second cup of coffee, I am sure I would find the experience very upsetting. It would violate my sense of reality so dramatically I would probably begin to question my sanity. During a dream, however, we experience what is called "dream logic." The regular rules of logic do not apply. Flying into the kitchen in a dream can be as acceptable to the dreamer as a walk in the park.

Young children have the ability to shift back and forth between the rules of reality and the rules of fantasy while awake. This is the essence of childhood imagination. Here again, we see the utility of a dream logic response to an extreme threat. When all else fails, and we are completely out of options, what better strategy than to gain access to that part of the mind able to think "outside the box." When it comes to survival, all options are on the table.

The brain's ability to compartmentalize awareness is an essential feature of consciousness. Just as sea mammals compartmentalize sleeping and waking consciousness between the hemispheres, in a less dramatic way, our brains are naturally partitioned into many separate systems, subsystems and clusters of associated, yet distinct facets of consciousness. Each aspect of consciousness is induced by and emerges from the signal transfer patterns of groups of neurons differentially activated as the billions of neurons in the brain play out their various states of conscious experience.

Many believe we can think only one thought at a time. This may be true for the nematode worm, but for humans, there is always much more going on all the time. The stream of thought we routinely experience as reality is just the surface layer of a vast multi-faceted ever-shifting cascading awareness emerging from the many contemporaneous expressions of signal transfer induced consciousness. Each facet of overt awareness is experienced as the next event briefly surfacing and then being quickly supplanted by the next emerging conscious experience. Like a movie reel of images stitched together to give the illusion of animation, our awareness is stitched together from the myriad of brain states giving rise to the flow of conscious experience.

This has significant implications for mental health. It suggests everything we sense; even those things below our "conscious" level of awareness influence our consciousness. Consciousness, like everything else, is a dynamic, transitional and relational process. All of our perceptions connect with, yet are momentarily dissociated from all other expressions of consciousness.

Evidence supporting this model of multiple simultaneous thought comes from thousands of peer-reviewed studies using hundreds of paradigms including research exploring the latency time for memory retrieval. If I were to ask you the color of your first bicycle, it would take a certain amount of time to access the information from memory. If I were to ask again an hour later, it would take less time to access the same information. Additionally, it would then take less time to access memories associated with (neurally connected to) your first bicycle memories. Maybe the bicycle was a Christmas gift received when you were five years old. After recalling the bike memory, you would then have faster access to all associated memories. That the system works in this way suggests some intermediate state of partitioned awareness operating below the current level of conspicuous consciousness. Like bubbles below the surface, representing separate yet associated compartments of potential conscious awareness.

Dissociative Identity Disorder (DID), sometimes mistakenly called multiple personality disorder, is a dramatic example of the capacity for the compartmentalization of consciousness. There is some controversy surrounding DID probably due to errors in over-diagnosis. Despite this controversy, it is clear the human mind compartmentalizes awareness and that DID is an extreme example of this compartmentalization.

Dissociated Identity Disorder usually occurs in response to severe psychological trauma. So like the tonic immobility response, DID is related to activation of the autonomic nervous system. Childhood traumas are more likely to induce DID than events occurring later in life because young minds can shift more readily between the rules of logic and the rules of fantasy. It is as if during a traumatic event, the young mind says to itself, "this experience is just too horrible to bear. You deal with it; I'm going over here where it is safe." According to the theory, a psychological partition emerges, and distinct personalities develop within each partition.

Patients with Dissociative Identity Disorder can develop several different characters. Often, the patient's "regular" character is unaware of the others until distress results in treatment. They are, after all, dissociated. The therapist is tipped off by dramatic shifts in a patient's mannerisms combined with other incongruent presentations. Reports of lost blocks of time and the discovery of strange clothing of an inconsistent style in the patient's wardrobe can add confidence to a diagnosis. DID personalities can be so distinct as to present with different physiologies.

When an actor assumes the role of a character, the player sometimes experiences the role as an altered state of consciousness. This is the difference between playing the part and being the part. The ability to "be the part" seems to occur more naturally with actors who create their own characters. The character becomes a partitioned aspect of the artist's psyche.

Almost everyone who grew up in North America in the last century knows the voice of Mel Blanc. He was the voice actor and creator of Bugs Bunny, Porky Pig, and Tweety Bird and over a thousand other beloved cartoon characters. In 1961 Mel was in a terrible car accident which left him comatose. He was completely unresponsive. Two weeks into the coma a neurologist entered Mel's hospital room, and instead of addressing Mel directly, he said, "Bugs Bunny, how are you doing today?" To which Mel weakly replied as Bugs Bunny, "Meeya, what's up Doc?"

Mel couldn't direct his attention to initiate communication as Mel because of the trauma to his brain, but the partitioned personality called Bugs Bunny was able to respond. It may be the partitioned associations of Bugs Bunny's awareness allowed access to critical neurological pathways allowing Mel's consciousness to begin to heal. As astonishing as this all sounds, Bugs Bunny may have saved Mel's life that day!

Let's think again about the compare-and-contrast process of categorization. Everything hinges on everything else. All consciousness is relational; context is essential for understanding. In this model, a positive comparison between two concepts is the process of saying "yes" to being included in the same category.

From a data processing perspective, association is the process of assigning "is" or "equals" between concepts. The two concepts then combine to form a new category of understanding. The new pattern of dynamic, transitional and relational signal transfer which emerges from the newly connected neurological association network now induces a new consciousness arising from the activation of the previously unassociated groups of neurons. Stimulating one cluster now tends to activate the other cluster. As far as the brain is concerned, "this" now equals "that" within the current context.

Adding new information to create a new category of understanding is very useful as we try to understand the relationships between concepts being considered. Bear equals danger; smile equals friendly, fire equals pain, these associations help us succeed.

Now consider the situation when two concepts are not associated. For instance, "viper" usually does not equal "snuggle." All concepts (except reflex and instinct) are unassociated by default. Some unassociated concepts have been evaluated and are known to not belong in the same category; others have yet to be evaluated at all. For efficiency, it is useful to distinguish between unevaluated and explicitly excluded pairs of concepts. In the absence of this, previously evaluated pairs of concepts would need evaluation every time they come up. It is much more efficient to explicitly dissociate concepts known to not belong in the same category. This process is the "contrast" function of the compare and contrast model of understanding.

From a data processing perspective, it is inefficient to be required to assess, reassess, and reevaluate again, ad infinitum, items found to be unassociated with each other within a particular context. Dissociation is the biological contrast function of information processing. For understanding to be both thorough and efficient, we need to be able to associate items which belong together while dissociating items which do not. Compare and contrast, "well that is all there is."

Consider the concept: "ball." Many items fit into this category. There are tennis balls, soccer balls, footballs, baseballs, etc. So the concept "ball," in this context, includes many different but similar items all having to do with sports. If I were to describe a social event wherein people wear evening attire specified on the invitation as "black tie" and in which formal dance makes up a large part of the night's activities, you would probably recognize that here too I was referring to a "ball." So here we have two categories which are the same in name, yet very different in other properties.

Most dissociations are passive because categories of understanding are by default unassociated. In the absence of learning or developmentally installed associations, clusters of potential awareness tend to have no association. Because the categories "bouncing ball" and "dancing ball" have no association in my mind other than the name (as far as I know) these two groups are passively dissociated for me in all other contexts. Categories with only a superficial association such as "dancing ball" and "bouncing ball" tend to require more time and effort to parse because their analysis requires the comparison of additional categories of understanding to sort it all out as we try to make sense of the similarities and differences.

There are times, however, when swift analysis can mean the difference between life and death. In these cases, passive dissociation will not due. Without an explicit dissociation, unassociated items would need processing from scratch every time. The partitions of consciousness seen in DID and to a lesser extent in Post Traumatic Stress Disorder (PTSD) are examples of an explicit "not in this category" dissociation. In these cases, attention gets partitioned through the inhibition of dissociated clusters of awareness within a given context. The inhibitory interneuron described earlier as part of the patella reflex which sent a signal to the opposing muscle group inhibiting contraction is a clear example of the system's capacity to express dissociation.

Association and dissociation are the functional

equivalents to compare and contrast making up bricks and mortar of biological information processing. Attention can now be described as the dynamic, transitional and relational signal transfer pattern of a cluster of neurons dissociated from, for the moment, all other groups of neurons producing other patterns of signal transfer which express other conscious states. We have indeed come a long way towards understanding the nature of consciousness.

The question now becomes; just how does a system able to experience an infinite number of possible conscious states decide where and when to direct attention? Once again, nature provides the answer. The chapter on motivation described reflex, instinct, and instinctively motivated drives as being the primary motivators of behavior. Toward that end, the ultimate authority for command and control of consciousness is the autonomic nervous system. The autonomic nervous system ensures survival by regulating vital physiologic functions and having ultimate authority for directing our attention.

Processing the most salient survival based information available is the autonomic nervous system's primary function. When it is activated, all other considerations are, for the moment, partitioned apart from active consciousness. We see an example of this preeminent autonomic control of consciousness in PTSD.

PTSD is a trauma-induced disorder characterized by hyper vigilance towards stimuli not ordinarily considered to be threatening. This hyper-vigilance is a relatively rigid dissociation of awareness away from the more normal states of consciousness.

The next priority level for directing human attention are the instinctively motivated drives for safety and security, socialization and sex. These states of consciousness result from a negotiation between the autonomic nervous system and the higher level neocortex expectations of change in pain and pleasure. These systems make up the survival based operating system of consciousness. Though they usually operate below "conscious" level of awareness, they are always "on the air" influencing thought and behavior.

Case in point; not long ago I was out for an early morning jog when I was attacked by a swarm of bees. The experience was terrifying. I have not run that fast since high school, and I was only able to escape by jumping into the back of a stranger's pickup truck.

Knowing something of PTSD, I made every effort to thoroughly process the experience by discussing it with pretty much anybody who would listen. I even tracked down the location of the hive from the safety of my car so that I could report the danger to the city. Later, the postman told me the bees had been removed, after he told me his own horrific story.

About a week later, I decided to take an early morning bike ride. I remember enjoying the ride and feeling particularly happy and carefree. Not a cloud on the horizon. As I came to a scenic portion of the journey where a canopy of overarching trees framed the roadway, I suddenly experienced a dramatic and surprising shift in my consciousness. My serenity was abruptly jolted into a state of panic as I noticed something moving just inches away from my face. By the time I figured out it was only a leaf fallen from a tree, my system was in a full-blown fight or flight panic alert. My heart was pounding, and I felt the same terror I experienced the week before during the bee attack. My thoughts raced back to the memory of the event. Here is a likely explanation for my exaggerated reaction to a falling leaf.

Different groups of neurons express different patterns of signal transfer induced consciousness. Each cluster of neurons connects with many other clusters, but not all groups associate equally with each other. Some clusters, especially those responsible for processing vital survival functions, have a more direct access to the autonomic fight or flight system than others. The neurons inducing awareness of the meaning of the word "gun," for instance, have a more direct association with the autonomic nervous system than the cluster of neurons producing meaning of the word "banana."

We can think of clusters of neurons as being like locations on a map. Some locations have many connections with other locations while others have only a few links to other sites. Those with only a few associations are like the side streets and cul-de-sacs of awareness. Highly interconnected clusters reflect a more detailed understanding of the concepts under consideration. These are like villages and hamlets with many interconnected pathways.

In this analogy, the rigid dissociations of PTSD and DID function like the borders of divided cities with the reduced connection between partitions. When concepts and understandings between dissociated regions fail to connect, we see the potential for conflicting irrational beliefs from within the same brain. This absence of integrity or "oneness" results from differences in the context of partitioned structures. Each conflicted belief structure resides in a dissociated system of awareness reflecting a different context for the conflicted understanding. Psychotherapy seeks to integrate these areas of conflicted consciousness.

Each facet of conscious awareness is a potential voice in the choir of overall conscious experience. There are always many melodies, harmonies, rhythms, and counter-rhythms being played out all the time in the music hall of our mind.

And now we see how a leaf falling from a tree on a beautiful, carefree morning bike ride can produce a state of panic in someone getting over a bee attack. Though my overt consciousness was seemingly at ease enjoying the ride, just below the surface many other clusters of awareness were on high alert monitoring the environment for signs of trouble.

These groups of neurons were on guard having been primed by the bee attack a week earlier. The neurons which process visual movement and object proximity tend to be particularly primal and are therefore well-connected to the fight or flight response circuits (think reptiles and predation). As the falling leaf entered my field of view close to my face with a motion similar to that of an insect, a flood of signals propagated throughout my nervous system causing the entire choir of subconscious awareness to sing out loud "EMERGENCY!"

PTSD is nature's way of limiting our responses to only those behaviors most likely to result in survival in light of experience. The dissociations of PTSD reduce wasted time and motion when time and motion matter most. Also, it seems likely that sleep in general and REM, in particular, play a critical role in the installation of dissociation circuits. These circuits customize our emergency response systems. Deep sleep cycles with intense dreams often follow stressful experiences. During these dream sleep cycles, the brain is running cognitive simulations in order to customize our new emergency response association networks.

It is no coincidence we see the emergence of dissociation at about the same point in evolutionary development as sleeping behavior. Sleeping is dissociation from waking consciousness. Recall the fish Nimbochromis described earlier. It lies on the bottom and assumes a blotchy coloration to lure scavengers to within striking distance. We noted how few things could be more stimulating to a hungry fish than the presentation of food. From this excited state, we see an early form of something like tonic immobility.

For the behavioral choice between fight, flight and tonic immobility to increase the probability of survival, the fish must somehow model an accurate prediction of likely outcomes for each of the different potential behaviors within the current context. The fish must be engaged in an early form of reflective consciousness. It is only by successfully predicting outcomes at a rate greater than random chance that the fish actually increases the probability of survival. When this happens, the trait of reflective consciousness gets passed on. Consciousness is a naturally emergent process.

Effective cognitive modeling of behavior requires the same context for both the cognitions and the event being modeled. When striking prey, timing is essential. The mental simulations of behavior should, therefore, play out with the same autonomic activation as the striking action itself. And now we see why the real-time autonomic REM state becomes a logical evolutionary adaptation for the increased complexity of reflective consciousness. It is REM dissociation that allows the organism to strategize between fight, flight or tonic immobility modeled within a real-time autonomic survival context. Once again, survival is the driving force.

This all lines up nicely with other observations on "knowing" and "learning." The simple nervous system of the roundworm C. Elegans can learn through classical conditioning to avoid a previously attractive stimulus. With the development of dissociation and the ability to cognitively model outcomes, we see for the first time the capacity for more advanced operant like conditioning.

During the classical conditioning of reflex behaviors, the environment is acting on the organism. With the development of dissociation and the capacity to cognitively model various possible behaviors, we see the emergence of operant conditioning as the organism seems to act on the environment.

With three mutually exclusive potential responses to a challenge, the organism now really has something to "think" about. Fight, flight or tonic immobility; choosing one excludes, for the moment, selecting the others. The organism must decide and survival hangs in the balance.

Both fight and flight are similar in that they are both highly motivated directed action. The difference is the direction of the effort. In the fight mode, the organism directs action towards the challenge while in the flight mode it directs attention away from the challenge. These responses are very different from the tonic immobility response. Here, nature has brought something new, the compartmentalization of consciousness.

Up to this point, we have been describing consciousness in a very deterministic way. Reflex and conditioned response suggests no choice in the behavior and therefore no "self" and for that matter, no moral culpability. Before the dissociation function, all behavior is easily seen as the result of cause and effect. There does not seem to be any free will at all. For the will to be free, the actor must have the ability to act as well as the ability to not act. Free will must include both free will and "free won't." With the development of dissociation, we see for the first time a consciousness able to choose between behaviors,… maybe.

Stickgold, R. (2005) Nature 437, 1272-1278 (27 October 2005) Sleep-dependent memory consolidation

Oleg I. L, Manger P, Ridgway S, Mukhametov L, Siegel J Neuroscience and Biobehavioral Reviews 32 (2008) 1451–1484 Cetacean sleep: An unusual form of mammalian sleep

McNamara P., Auerbach S., Johnson P., Harris E., Doros G. Journal of Affective Disorders, May 2010 Volume 122, Issue 3, Pages 198–207 Impact of REM sleep on distortions of self-concept, mood and memory in depressed/anxious participants

7 COMMUNICATION

Communication is signal transfer which alters consciousness. Since human consciousness emerges most directly from the dynamic, transitional and relational signal transfer patterns between neurons in the brain, human communication occurs when signal transmission alters the dynamic, transitional and relational signal transfer patterns between neurons in the human brain.

Now the nervous system is clearly a physical structure. It interacts with other physical structures in strict accordance with the immutable laws of chemistry and physics. Consciousness, on the other hand, does not directly interact with either physical matter or the consciousness of other systems. For this reason, all communication must be expressed as physical signals.

When different nervous systems are similarly "attuned," they tend to respond to similar signals in a similar way. This phenomenon can create the illusion of direct communication between minds. The illusion is so strong they even have a name for it. They call it telepathy.

A recent New York Times poll found 57% of Americans believed in psychic phenomena like telepathy. This enduring yet completely unsubstantiated belief has led to decades of research looking for evidence of telepathy. In spite of all these efforts, there are no scientifically valid studies supporting the direct communication between minds.

If valid scientific evidence for telepathy were found it would capture worldwide attention and stagger the scientific community. There would be a flurry of new research hoping to exploit the new findings. It is no exaggeration to say valid scientific evidence for telepathy would be the news of the century. Now it is impossible to prove the nonexistence of anything, however, because of the strong motivational forces involved, the absence of evidence for telepathy is pretty compelling evidence for the absence of telepathy.

We can add confidence to this position by considering how telepathy would influence evolution. If direct communication between minds were operative, evolution would have favored a very different nervous system. Remember nature is extremely efficient. With telepathy, there would be no need for the costly allocation of nerves and muscles for facial expression and body language. Also, direct communication between minds would make many aspects of language obsolete. Deception would be impossible.

Now, it is true electromagnetic fields can induce other electromagnetic fields. It may even be that the electrochemical activity in one part of a brain interacts with other nearby structures through electromagnetic field induction. One can imagine the weak electromagnetic fields produced by depolarizing and repolarizing clusters of neurons perhaps influencing other nearby structures. This may even play an important as yet undiscovered role in consciousness. Even so, there is a good reason to doubt field induction could facilitate direct communication between minds.

Even if electromagnetic field induction could influence consciousness directly, the effect would fall off sharply as the distance between structures increases due to the inverse square law governing the strength of all electromagnetic fields. Double the distance and the field strength weakens by a factor of four, triple the distance and the field strength weakens nine-fold. Also, if consciousness could be affected by electromagnetic fields, the cacophony of electromagnetic radiation emanating from everything from cell phones to kitchen appliances would tend to scramble thoughts. Since thought seems unaffected by these much more powerful fields, electromagnetic field induction as a mechanism for telepathic communication does not seem likely. Yes, based on what we know about the universe, it seems safe to say there is no direct communication between minds.

Human consciousness emerges most directly from the dynamic, transitional and relational signal transfer patterns between clusters of neurons in the human brain. There are many ways to encode a message for communication, but because the fabric of human consciousness emerges from patterns of signal transfer between neurons in the brain, the encoding and decoding of all communication begins and ends as signal transfer patterns between neurons in the brain.

The messages of communication can be expressed as either chemical signals (scent and taste), auditory signals, tactile signals or visual signals. These signals are then detected by the sensory organ systems of the receiver of the message which decodes the message thereby altering the signal transfer patterns of the receiver's nervous system.

The simplest form of communication in nature occurs through chemical messaging sensed as scent or taste. Ants, for instance, after finding food, communicate the path leading back to the food to other ants by laying down a chemical trail as they return to the colony. When other ants detect this chemical message, they follow the path. If they find food, they add to the chemical trail as they also return. When the food source is exhausted, the chemical message dissipates. This chemical messaging system increases efficiency.

Like all communication, ant communication alters

consciousness. Whenever the "follow the path" chemical signal is received, the nervous system receiving the signal shifts into the "follow the path" neurological activation pattern. This change in consciousness results in "follow the path" behavior. When the chemical message dissipates, the neurological activation pattern shifts again and behavior changes to reflect a new state of ant consciousness. Ant communication alters ant consciousness.

The nervous system of the ant is relatively simple. It can experience several states of "ant consciousness." Each state of ant consciousness corresponds to a specific set of behaviors. Foraging for food is a state of consciousness associated with foraging behaviors. Following a chemical path is a state of ant consciousness related to following the path actions. Nest maintenance is a state of consciousness related to nest maintenance behaviors. Defending the nest is a state of consciousness associated with defending the nest behavior, and the list goes on. Each state of ant consciousness results from the ant's neurological activation pattern which is directly responsible for inducing the associated set of behaviors.

The chemical messages which alter consciousness act something like the executive activation command of a computer program. Activating the program initiates a series of stimulus and response neurological circuits. Each chemically encoded command specifies the behavioral program to be run. All healthy ants have these neurological behavior programs instinctively built into their nervous systems.

Let's say a colony is engaged in nest maintenance. That is to say; the ants are experiencing a state of consciousness which results in nest maintenance behaviors. When an intruder disrupts the colony, ants detecting the threat release a chemical message to alert the colony. This volatile compound vaporizes rapidly and spreads widely to induce a dramatic shift in ant colony consciousness. When detected, the ants shift into the "defend the nest" behavior pattern. As far as the ant's nervous system is concerned, chemical message equals defend the nest actions.

Like bacteria becoming resistant to antibiotic challenge or a meadow of plants adjusting their chemistry in anticipation of insect attack, the ant colony is more than the sum of its parts. The system as a whole functions more intelligently and more adaptively than individual ants alone. Chemical messaging allows the colony to work something like a single integrated nervous system. When ants are networked together in this way, the colony exhibits greater emergent intelligence as evidenced by the ability to defend against threats more effectively.

When insect neurons are networked together within an ant nervous system, we see emergent intelligence expressed by ant behaviors reflecting the various states of ant consciousness. When these systems are then networked together into an ant colony, we see the emergence of ant colony consciousness with enhanced intelligence able to coordinate tasks like nest building, rearing the young, finding food and defending the nest. With each new layer of complexity; ant neuron, ant nervous system, ant colony, we see increasing emergent intelligence approaching something like integrated consciousness.

Chemical messaging allows for simple patterns of consciousness; however, there is no "self" awareness in a system like this. Ant colonies do not write books about ant colony consciousness. Chemical communication alone lacks the subjective nuanced abstract representations of "reality" required for self-conscious awareness.

Chemical communication is insufficient for self-awareness because chemical messages are too objective and too deterministic. Each chemical compound corresponds with one state of consciousness leading to one set of behaviors. One chemical compound equals food trail, and a different chemical compound equals defend the nest. The precise nature of chemical compounds means there is little chance for error, but it also means there is little chance for innovation. Chemical messaging systems are too rigid.

Bees also communicate using chemical signals, but bees have an additional way to send and receive information. Bees also communicate through their behavior. Communication encoded as behavior is a significant step forward in the development of consciousness. It allows bees to fine-tune their messages to better meet the needs of an ever-changing world.

Bees not only communicate the presence of food, they can also express flight instructions for finding the food. This behaviorally coded communication system is called the "waggle dance," and it dramatically increases food gathering efficiency.

That these creatures can abstractly encode, express, and interpret navigation information from dance behavior is astonishing. On the face of it, it seems almost magical. Just imagine a happy bee dancing back in the hive after finding a rich supply of nectar, perhaps thinking something like, "I had such a good day today finding all that delicious nectar just over the hill towards the east about a mile away." Then, another bee, observing all this starts to think, "Wow look how happy that bee is. He must be having a really good day. I wonder where he found all that nectar. He's dancing as if he found it towards the east about a mile away."

Obviously, bees do not think in this way. There is a long way to go before consciousness becomes this complex. Behaviorally coded communication, however, reflects an important step forward in the progression of consciousness because behaviorally coded messages are very different from chemically coded messages.

Chemically coded messages work through direct physical contact between the chemical signal and the organism receiving the message. Scent, for example, is experienced when olfactory receptors detect the chemical compound being sensed causing a chemical reaction within the receptor cell resulting in depolarization ultimately shifting the neurological activation pattern of the organism having the experience. The altered neurological activation pattern is the change in consciousness associated with detecting the scent. Taste operates in much the same way. With sight, sound and touch, however, the sensory organ system has no direct physical contact with the object being sensed.

Instead, signals of light and/or pressure mediate these behaviorally coded messages. The waggle dance of the bee is encoded primarily through the medium of light. Light is electromagnetic radiation. The light reflected off a waggle dancer stimulates the visual sensory system of the observer causing depolarization of the receptor cells in the observer's eye. These depolarizations are then transmitted to the nervous system and ultimately experienced as the altered state of perceiving the dance.

Similarly, sound waves are mediated by acoustic signals sensed by the auditory receptors of the ear depolarizing in response to pressure changes in the air set in motion by the vibration of the object heard. And the sense of touch is mediated through pressure and temperature receptors cells within the tissues depolarizing in response to changes in pressure and temperature of the skin. Sight, sound and touch sensations occur through the visual, auditory and tactile sensory organ systems. The sensory organ systems undergo electrochemical change in response to the mediated signals which then alter the neurological activation pattern of the nervous system having the experience.

With the chemical messaging of taste and scent, the neurochemistry and neurological activation pattern gets altered directly by the chemical message itself. With sight, sound and touch mediated communications, the neurochemistry and neurological activation pattern are changed indirectly by the sensory organ systems of the receiver of the message. It just is the function of sensory organ systems to alter consciousness in response to sensation.

Both direct chemical communication and sensory organ mediated communication alter consciousness, but there is an important difference between these two modes of sensation. Because chemical compounds are distinct, each alters neurological activation in a very objective way. Sight, sound and touch sensory organ mediated communication, on the other hand, is more subjective because the same stimulus will be interpreted differently depending on the perspective of the observer. Sensory organ mediated communication introduces context into the process of sensation.

Also, sensory organ mediated communication adds an additional layer of coding complexity. With this new layer of complexity, we see new opportunities for variance in the message. Behaviorally coded messages are more abstract and subjective than chemically coded messages because sensory organ mediated messages are in effect messages about messages.

Anyone familiar with the childhood game "telephone" knows how messages about messages can be a tricky business. Messages about messages often result in a shifted interpretation of the original stimuli. To appreciate just how these differences come about we need to understand the physics of sensory organ mediated communication.

Here is an all too brief and thoroughly incomplete description of the process of seeing the color red. Visual messages come in the form of light either emitted by or reflected from the object seen. Light is electromagnetic radiation. Humans see wavelengths of light ranging from about 360 to 760 nanometers. These wavelengths correspond to the colors of the visible spectrum; red, orange, yellow, green, blue, indigo and violet (ROYGBIV).

When light enters a human eye, receptor cells called rods and cones react. Rods are sensitive to a broad spectrum of wavelengths perceived as gray-scale. Cones are sensitive to more narrow bands of light and are seen as color. When stimulated, these cells undergo a chemical reaction changing the light energy into electrochemical signals as the receptor cells depolarize.

Humans have three types of cone cells differentially sensitive to red, green and blue wavelengths of light. The mantis shrimp, on the other hand, has twelve cone types allowing it to distinguish between many more colors of light than humans.

Each human eye has about 120 million rods and about 6 million cones connected to about a million nerve fibers in each optic nerve carrying the signals to the occipital lobes of the brain. Rods and cones react to light based on the light's wavelength, intensity, and location upon the retina.

Rods are more sensitive than cones because as many as 120 rods converge to a single optic nerve fiber while typically only six cones stimulate a single fiber. Each instant of visual sensation generates a vast stream of data from the sensing array providing much more information than any chemical compound could possibly communicate.

Because red light stimulates red-sensitive cone cells more

than green or blue sensitive cone cells, the signals generated by a retina sensing red light will be specific to red wavelengths. Red cone signals are then passed on by the optic nerve to the primary visual cortex altering the neurochemistry and neurological activation pattern of color resonating neurons in the occipital lobes. These signals then propagate to associated groups of neurons throughout the cortex. Compare and contrast operations take place between the various association networks experiencing the change in consciousness. The change in the neurological activation of clusters of neurons able to resonate with red color awareness just is the shift in consciousness associated with the perception of seeing the color red.

This very brief description does not include the many reflections and reverberations of consciousness which occur throughout the brain in response to all perceptual experiences. The language processing centers, for instance, might resonate with awareness of the word "red." Depending on the context, this may induce any number of potential associations ranging from warm, loving Saint Valentine's Day hearts to bloody murder victims. If the percipient has experienced a "red" associated trauma, perhaps something to do with a fire truck, the sympathetic nervous system may become activated. Sensory experiences can trigger any number of associated neurological activation patterns based on history and development.

Since there is no direct contact with the stimulus sensed during sensory organ system mediated communication, the message is an abstract representation of the object or event being detected. The signals are a "reflection" of reality. When an organism communicates through behavior, the visual signals detected by the receiver are an abstract representation of the behavior which is an abstract representation of the consciousness to be induced. We see this with the waggle dance of the bee abstractly representing navigation information.

The bee's communication requires a one-to-one correspondence between abstract representation of reality and the reality the abstract representation is intended to reflect. Each set of waggle dance behaviors must correspond to one particular set of flight instructions leading to one specific location relative to the hive. A different set of dance steps represents a different set of flight instructions resulting in a different journey. This communication of abstract representations of reality to induce a particular state of consciousness is best explained as a form of "sympathetic resonance" between nervous systems.

In physics, the sympathetic resonance of sound is the phenomenon whereby an object at rest begins to vibrate in response to the vibration of a different object to which it is harmonically attuned. To understand how this works we need to understand the physics of sound. Sound is sensed primarily through sensory receptors in the ear. Loud sounds can also be detected by pressure receptor cells in the tissues, but here we will focus only on the sensations of the ear.

Strike a bell, and the bell vibrates. The strike deforms the physical structure of the bell causing it to oscillate back and forth in an elastic like fashion. These oscillations cause the air molecules adjacent to the bell to move back and forth generating cascading waves of air molecule oscillations. These cascading air molecule oscillations cause the eardrum to oscillate back and forth. As the eardrum vibrates in response to the oscillation of adjacent air molecules set in motion by the bell, the sound energy is ultimately transmitted to tiny hair-like structures in the inner ear. These structures vary in length and act like an array of tuning forks selectively vibrating according to the frequency or pitch being heard. These frequency specific vibrations are then transformed into electrochemical energy as the attached auditory receptor cells depolarize in response. The signals are then carried along the cochlear nerve to the temporal lobes altering the neurological activation pattern which is ultimately experienced as hearing the sound.

Humans can detect vibrations ranging from about 20 to 20,000 cycles per second. Differences in frequency are sensed as differences in pitch. Middle "C" on the piano, for instance, vibrates at 261 cycles per second while the note "A" above middle "C" vibrates at 440 cycles per second. Different species can hear different sound wave frequencies. Dogs can hear up to 60,000 cycles per second and elephants can sense sound as low as 14 cycles per second.

The classic example of sympathetic vibration occurs when a singer breaks a wine glass using only the sound energy of the singing voice. Here is how it works. Every object has a natural resonance or frequency to which it is naturally "tuned." If you strike a wine glass, a musical pitch occurs defined by the frequency of its vibration. The tone occurs due to the physical structure and composition of the object. Identical glasses have the same harmonic properties and resonate with the same pitch when struck. A wine glass at rest exposed to the sound frequency to which it is naturally attuned it will absorb the sound energy and begin to vibrate in response. This reaction is called sympathetic vibration. If the sound energy is intense enough, it will shatter the glass.

Like identical wine glasses, bees have similarly tuned nervous systems each with the ability to sympathetically "resonate" with the different states of bee consciousness. When a bee performs a waggle dance, it is in a state of consciousness corresponding to "awareness" of the flight behaviors leading to a particular location of nectar. When other bees observe the dance, a similar state of "knowledge" gets sympathetically induced. The nervous system of the observer becomes attuned to the nervous system of the dancer thereby producing awareness of the flight behaviors leading to the nectar.

That nervous systems can experience induced states of consciousness is an intuitively attractive idea that has important implications for human consciousness. It is further evidence suggesting that consciousness just is a function of the dynamic, transitional, relational signal transfer patterns between neurons. That is to say, consciousness is experienced as, and explained by the moment to moment physical chemistry and neurological activation pattern of the system having the conscious experience.

Researchers have decoded the waggle dance. Each dance sequence begins at a particular starting position on the honeycomb. The bee moves forward "wagging" the tail end of its body back and forth as it goes. After a traversing a prescribed distance, the bee then circles back around to the starting point and repeats the process. It alternates between circling back to the left and circling back to the right thereby forming a figure eight pattern as it repeats the dance. The angle of the forward motion relative to the honeycomb corresponds to the flight heading relative to the position of the sun thereby inducing flight heading awareness.

Distance information correlates with the forward motion portion of the dance. I have a theory for the mechanics underlying waggle dance distance communication which lines up nicely with other observations of consciousness. I did not find a description of this mechanism in my cursory search, so this may be the first publication of the idea.

The theory goes like this: all creatures have cycles or rhythms to which they are naturally attuned. Circadian rhythms, for instance, are the daily cycles regulating metabolism, feeding, and sleep. There are regular periods associated with heart rate, respiratory rate, and digestive peristalsis. Insects demonstrate rhythmic patterns evidenced by the sounds of crickets and the flashing of fireflies. Yes, all nature is rhythmically attuned.

Now, for a bee to maintain a flight heading relative to the sun would require periodic course assessment and correction. It is reasonable to assume a bee would cycle through regular intervals of course evaluation and correction during the flight. It is also sensible to believe that bees experiencing similar flight conditions will tend to travel at about the same speed and assess heading at about the same rate.

We know the direction of the waggle dance relative to the honeycomb corresponds to flight heading relative to the angle of the sun, and we also know distance correlates with the duration of the forward motion portion of the dance. It is my theory each waggle of the waggle dance reflects a cycle of course assessment and correction.

If true, it now becomes more clear how the waggle dance actually works. What at first appears to be a thoroughly abstract representation of reality can now be seen as the acting out in dance of the actual flight behaviors necessary to find the nectar. The waggle dance is a form of behavioral programming through demonstration. The waggle dancer is saying travel in this direction for this many course correction cycles and you will find the nectar.

My theory lines up nicely with other ideas about dissociation and altered states of consciousness. For a bee to recall and demonstrate a previous flight memory requires the bee to direct attention internally. This internal focus is a dissociation from external awareness similar to the dissociation of sleep. In effect, the waggle dance is like a waking dream reliving the flight to the nectar.

Recall that humans dream in two ways. During autonomic REM sleep, dreams play out in real time, however during non-REM sleep; dreams play out in compressed time. The very good news of finding an abundant supply of nectar is not a "fight or flight" like experience. So the non-autonomic waking dream of the waggle dance unfolds in compressed time as the actual behaviors leading to the nectar. It is the simplest and most efficient way to communicate the information. It all just makes sense!

Human nervous systems also become sympathetically aligned through modeling of behavior in a similar induction like process. We regularly experience induced moods of empathy, joy, anger, fear and sexual arousal as we interact with others, especially those with whom we are similarly attuned. There are many modes through which sympathetic induction of consciousness can take place including facial expressions, body language, and tone of voice. And like insects and plants, we can resonate with others through the chemical communication of taste and scent as well.

The nervous systems of similar creatures tend to resonate in similar ways when exposed to similar inductive experiences. Our response to music is a good example of the way nervous systems can become sympathetically attuned. The Adagio in G Minor will almost always induce a sweetly sad and deeply reverent state of consciousness in all who listen. This effect seems to hold true across time and culture suggesting the music somehow taps into something fundamental about the human nervous system. The structure of the nervous system causes it to be emotionally moved by the experience. And not just the human nervous system; they say: "music hath charms to soothe the savage beast." The nervous systems of all mammals have much in common. Similar nervous systems resonate in similar ways in response to similar inductive experiences.

It is also true all nervous systems differ. In some ways, every nervous system is unique. The ideas of sympathetic resonance can also account for individual differences as well. The differences between nervous systems can be thought of in the same way as differences between musical instruments. Each instrument has a unique voice based on the structure and composition of the instrument, and the performance patterns of the player. These differences combine to generate variations in the harmonic overtones of each instrument.

Most sounds in nature are intricate. They are composed of many frequencies all occurring at the same time. Pure tones, like those of a tuning fork, are rare. A pure tone generates a smooth sine wave pattern when graphed. Complex tones, on the other hand, look more like a jagged seismograph. The sound of a saxophone and the sound of a French horn each playing the same note differ due to the harmonic overtones "folded" into the tone.

The human voice and the sound of waves crashing against the shore are examples of complex sounds containing many simultaneous harmonic overtones. Our ability to identify others by the sound of their voice is due to the nervous system's ability to recognize the differences and similarities of harmonic overtone patterns. Not only can we identify the speaker, we can usually identify the mood and the level of arousal based solely on the acoustics of their voice. The human auditory processing system is so well-developed most people can distinguish between the sound of hot and cold water poured into identical cups.

When we say humans are social creatures, this is just another way of saying we can become sympathetically attuned to each other. There will always be differences between individuals, but as social beings, all healthy humans have the ability to become psychologically attuned with others. The closest and most comfortable associations occur between people with similarly tuned nervous systems expressing similar "harmonic overtone" patterns allowing for easy transitions between states of consciousness.

The advertising and entertainment industries sell the sympathetic induction of consciousness. Culture itself is a means of tuning the nervous systems of the population. The Bible and Homer's Iliad and the Odyssey tune a nervous system differently than Taoism and Shintoism.

People with similarly tuned nervous systems tend to get along well while those with differently tuned nervous systems find close associations more challenging. If everybody understood the nature of consciousness, our nervous systems would become more naturally attuned to one another. Spread the word.

Now that we have a basic understanding of the signal transfer process we call communication the next chapter will look at the way the signals of communication are processed to generate the perceptions of consciousness.

8 PERCEPTION

Perception is the process of organizing and interpreting sensory signals. It is an interactive process. As the act of perception alters the neurological activation pattern inducing consciousness the perception will also change. So perception is the moment to moment shifting and re-aligning of consciousness in response to the sensory signals perceived. Just as "knowing" emerges from the awareness of the similarities and differences between things, perception emerges as clusters of neurons calculate the similarities and differences between sensation and the catalog of experience.

Human visual perception is a complex process. Each eye connects to the brain through an optic nerve with about one million neural connections. These two million data channels deliver an ever-changing signal stream first to the thalamus and then on to the primary visual cortex of the occipital lobes. During each moment of visual perception, billions of photons of light strike the retinas stimulating the hundreds of millions of rods and cones responsible for generating the two million channels of electrochemical visual data. It is almost too much to consider. Fortunately, the mind can conceive beyond its ability to perceive as demonstrated by the following thought experiment.

Almost everyone knows a triangle is a polygon with three sides. You may not know a chiliagon is a polygon with a thousand sides. The definition of a chiliagon allows most people to conceive of a chiliagon as effortlessly as a triangle. Though easily imagined, humans can not perceive chiliagons. The difference between the surface area of a chiliagon and a circle with the same radius is less than

0.0004 percent which is beyond the human eye's ability to distinguish. People see an entire chiliagon as a circle. Understanding the full complexity of human vision is like trying to visualize a chiliagon. To better appreciate the full complexity of visual information processing, we turn again to the natural world. Charting the evolution of vision across species to understand human visual perception it is little like starting with a triangle to grasp a chiliagon.

Some simple microorganisms have sensory organelles called eyespots with photoreceptor proteins able to distinguish between light and dark. The Euglena is a unicellular organism with properties of both plants and animals. Like plants, it uses light for photosynthesis, and like animals, it can move about and ingest nutrients directly. The Euglena has a primitive eyespot located at the base of its flagellum. Together, the flagella and eyespot allow it to move towards the light facilitating photosynthesis.

It is believed advances in visual sensing sparked the Cambrian Explosion, an evolutionary event 542 million years ago which saw a dramatic increase in the diversity of life. New sensing abilities fueled a veritable arms race between predator and prey. Survival pressures caused an "explosion" of evolutionary change. The fossil record from this period shows rapid development of visual sensing along with a dramatic increase in the diversity of life.

Flat eyespots evolved by forming an indentation or cup shape. The Planarian is a flatworm with cup-like eyespots able to slightly distinguish the direction of light. Flat eyespots can not determine the direction of light because light from any direction will stimulate the entire surface of a flat eye in the same way. Arranging the sensory cells into a cup shape allows shadows to be cast, so the receptor cells making up the cup will be differently stimulated based on the angle of light. This early form of proto-eye can detect the direction of light but still lacks the ability to resolve image shape. Over time as species developed, eye cups deepened and the number of receptor cells increased.

The addition of receptor cells in the sensing array increases image resolution. Also, each new receptor tends to correspond to new neural structure to handle the new data stream. With the addition of new neurological structures, we see an increase in the permutations of potential compare and contrast observation experiences. And so concurrent with the development of new visual processing we see the expansion of consciousness.

The eye of a sea nautilus functions like a pinhole camera. Here the eye spot has transitioned from eyespot to eye cup, to eye pit, and in the case of the sea nautilus, becoming an eye "chamber." The reduction in the size of the eye-opening allows light direction sensing and even simple shape resolution. With no cornea or lens to focus the image, the Nautilus has poor shape resolution and poor low light sensitivity. Even so, this configuration is a dramatic improvement over earlier eyespots and eye cups.

In nature, form follows function. Eye placement on the organism also influences performance. The eyes of prey are usually positioned on the sides of the head for the greatest field of view to avoid predators. Predators, on the other hand, tend to have their eyes located towards the front of the head resulting in a narrower field of view but offering improved depth perception crucial for precise attack. Creatures hoping to avoid predation have noted the correlation between eye placement and survival threat.

The nervous system is always "on the air" always seeking out patterns of similarities and differences affecting survival. Recognizing the correlation between eye placement and predatory behavior offers a significant survival advantage. After countless encounters over millions of years, the mammalian nervous system has developed specialized clusters of neurons within the visual processing centers able to calculate the spatial relationship of eye placement as a way of identifying threats. These threat detecting clusters of neurons connect with the autonomic fight or flight response system. When activated, they contribute a voice in the choir of risk assessment. Humans also have these specialized clusters of neurons so it should come as no surprise there is a correlation between human eye placement and the human sense of the aesthetic.

Most cultures consider eyes set wide apart to be a sign of innocence and beauty while narrow set eyes are considered less attractive and are associated with cunning predator like properties. Of course, there is no evidence to suggest human eye placement correlates with personality or temperament, but it is easy to see why these prejudices exist. Deep down inside, below our conscious level of awareness, for excellent reasons, the nervous system is just more at ease with relatively wide set eyes.

Color vision is another example of a specialized awareness induced by clusters of neurons able to resonate with specialized consciousness related to survival advantages. Many color specific behavior patterns have been identified. It is no coincidence we associate red with Saint Valentine's Day. Red flesh tones indicate health, fertility and a readiness to mate leading to healthy offspring. The response to red lips suggesting vitality and fertility is very different from the response to blue lips indicating insufficient oxygen to the tissues. Ripened fruits and freshly sprouted leaves are also more easily detected with color vision. In short, any information in the environment coded in color which offers a survival advantage is likely to have an associated compare and contrast neurological network designed to make use of the valuable information.

Now is a good time for a brief review of the physics of light. Perception of color is the sensing and processing of the similarities and differences between wavelengths of light. Light is electromagnetic radiation. It exists in the form of energy packets called photons. Light photons have properties of both waves and particles. There is a logical incongruence to wave-particle duality. It doesn't make sense that light can be both a wave and a particle, but that is what the evidence reliably indicates.

The human eye can detect wavelengths of light ranging from about 360 to 760 nanometers. We experience these wavelengths as the blended colors of the rainbow; red, orange, yellow, green, blue, indigo and violet. This spectrum of electromagnetic radiation extends in both directions beyond our ability to see. Infrared light is any light with a wavelength longer than red light. Radio waves and microwaves are examples of infrared light. Ultraviolet radiation is light with wavelengths shorter than violet light. X-rays and gamma rays are examples of ultraviolet radiation.

Different creatures see different wavelengths of light. Bees, for instance, see best in the ultraviolet range. Plants have evolved to take advantage of the ultraviolet vision of insects. Some flowers which appear to us to be a single color look very different when viewed in the ultraviolet. Many have what look like neon runways directing the insects to the nectar inside only visible to us when viewed using ultraviolet photography.

On the other end of the light spectrum, snakes sense infrared light through specialized stereoscopic organs located on their face. It is tempting to classify thermal radiation sensation and perception as touch since it is through touch that we sense the warmth of infrared radiation, but the snakes' infrared receptor signals get processed in the same area of the brain as visual signals suggesting this is more of a visual experience for the snake.

Most fish, all reptiles, and all birds have color vision. Mammals, except for a few primates and marsupials, are color blind. It is likely early mammals had color vision, but in becoming nocturnal during the reign of the dinosaurs, low light gray-scale vision offered greater survival advantages than color vision. For this reason, the redevelopment of color vision in some primates is unique in nature.

The retina is the light-sensitive layer of tissue on the inner surface of the eye lined with receptor cells called rods and cones. Rods are sensitive to a broad spectrum of low-intensity grayscale light useful for seeing at night while cones are sensitive to more narrowband colors in brighter daylight conditions. Humans usually have three different types of cones described as red, green and blue. Most other mammals have only green and blue cones. They do not see color in the same way as humans; they are color blind.

Color blindness is the inability to distinguish between specific wavelengths of light usually caused by the absence or malfunction of cone cells. There are many kinds of color blindness, but the most common in humans is due to the lack of red-sensitive cone cells usually caused by a mutation on the "X" chromosome. Males have a single instance of the "X" chromosome while females have two "X" chromosomes, so females have a built-in genetic color vision redundancy making female color blindness more rare. The chance of having the same flaw on both "X" chromosomes is small.

Understanding the development and mechanics of color

vision allows us to appreciate some fascinating research shedding light on the process of sensation, perception, and consciousness. To this point, we have focused mainly on the sensory aspect of color vision processing. We can now turn our attention downstream to some of the neurological processing associated with color vision perception, and the consciousness of seeing color.

Human visual perception is derived from the infinite permutations of the 252 million receptor cells of the retinas differentially responding to the various wavelengths of light entering the eyes. Most people see the color red and can easily distinguish it from other colors. They have all three types of receptor cones which when stimulated send color specific signals to clusters of neurons in the visual processing centers of the brain which are then able to resonate with color awareness. The perception of color just is the differential activation of these clusters of neurons inducing color consciousness. So the ability to see and recognize color is dependent upon both the presence of receptor cells on the retina and the associated neural clusters able to resonate with color awareness.

We are not born with the ability to experience color consciousness. The compare and contrast networks able to resonate with color consciousness arise from experience. A person blind from birth due to a defect of the lens would not see properly if the defect were corrected as an adult because the neural structures responsible for visual information processing in the brain would not have formed. These structures develop based on experience.

In a landmark study by Hubel and Wiesel (1963), cats had one eye sewn shut during the period between birth and three months of age. After reopening, vision in the affected eye never properly developed. Though the eye itself functioned normally, the neural networks of visual processing failed to develop without stimulation during critical periods of development. The new sensation data stream of the reopened eye had no neurological systems to activate. In contrast, adult cats with one eye sewn shut for up to a year regained normal vision after reopening the eye.

There are critical periods in the development of the nervous system during which the absence of normal stimulation results in neurological structures being utilized in other ways. Once a structure is reassigned, it is no longer available for its original intended purpose. It is as if these groups of neurons during certain critical periods of development demand to be engaged. If the system fails to provide the regular engagement, the structures find some other source of stimulation and develop another function to fulfill. For this reason, the treatment of color blindness in adults was thought to be impossible.

A study published in the journal Nature (Mancuso and colleagues, 2009) demonstrates the adult mammalian nervous system can learn to recognize newly-added red color sensory input. The study found monkeys were able to see previously undetectable red color after receiving gene therapy correcting a red cone cell deficiency causing their red-green color blindness.

The three types of cone cells in the human eye work together much like the three lamps of a projection color television system. Mixing the three colors allows for the full spectrum of normal human color vision. Blocking the red lamp of a projection television will simulate red-green color blindness. A red apple and a green apple will look the same to someone with red-green color blindness. It is the most common human genetic disorder occurring in 1 of 12 men and 1 of 230 women.

Male squirrel monkeys are naturally red-green colorblind. They lack the genetic code for making red cone receptors.

In collaboration with the laboratories at the University of Florida and the Medical College of Wisconsin, researchers at the Eye Institute of the University of Washington used a computerized test for color blindness on squirrel monkeys to assess color vision before and after gene therapy correcting a red cone cell deficiency. The gene therapy was applied using a virus injected into the retina to insert the missing genetic material. This treatment resulted in new red cone cells and ultimately in new red-green color vision.

Before treatment, the monkeys learned to touch patches of green and blue among gray dots on a touch-sensitive computer screen. This test for color vision is similar to the color vision testing books in which colored numbers or symbols are concealed within a pattern of gray dots. The monkeys received grape juice and a pleasant dinging sound for correct responses. Squirrel monkeys are very motivated by grape juice. A harsh buzzer tone followed incorrect responses. In this way, the monkeys were operantly conditioned to signal their perception of color.

Squirrel monkeys are color blind in the same way as humans with red-green color blindness. They lack red cone receptor cells. Following gene therapy, the monkeys were eventually able to demonstrate red color detection on the touch screen with ease. The researchers concluded; "A third type of cone pigment was added to dichromatic retinas, providing the receptoral basis for trichromatic color vision. Thus, trichromacy can arise from a single addition of a third cone class, and it does not require an early developmental process. This provides a positive outlook for the potential of gene therapy to cure adult vision disorders." This study offers us important insight into the perceptual mechanics of color vision.

All new learning, such as the ability to recognize a new color, is the creation of new neurological association networks in the brain. Learning just is the creation or altering of neural associations. The new red cone receptors formed new connections in the brain. These new connections then built new association networks eventually able to resonate with new red color awareness. These red aware structures then became associated with still other areas in the brain facilitating overt "consciousness" of red color awareness leading to new red color behavior at the touch screen and plenty of grape juice all around. All of this rewiring just is the learning process by which new color consciousness emerged.

Learning naturally occurs when the compare and contrast engine of consciousness combines with the motivation for survival. Before treatment, the monkeys saw colors in the same way as humans viewing a faulty projection television system missing the red lamp. The animals' nervous system already knew how to process signals from the green and blue receptors, but had no experience processing the new signals arriving in the brain from the newly added red receptors. These red cone signals were initially unrecognizable by the brain because the brain had no reliable history of compare and contrast experiences to draw upon for red color consciousness.

When the red signals began to arrive in the color processing areas of the brain, there was no distinct group of neurons able to resonate with red color awareness. Over time and experience, the nervous system was able to recognize a reliable correlation between red cone cell signals and specific objects within the visual field. In this way, the compare and contrast engine could begin to work its magic.

Pure color composed of a single wavelength of light is rare in nature. Lasers do emit a pure form of single wavelength light, but natural light almost always consists of many simultaneous wavelengths. Before treatment, red was seen as a sort of yellowish green/gray resulting from the signals of partially stimulated blue and green receptor cones mixed with the broad spectrum gray-scale signals generated by rod receptors. This began to change with the introduction of the new signals generated by the new red cone cells responding to red wavelengths of light.

The compare and contrast engine began to distinguish between red and non-red signals as a new catalog of color experience was being formed. Sometimes light from an image would be mostly green or mostly blue. These signals were already well "understood" by the color processing clusters of the brain. That is to say, these experiences already correlated well with the known catalog of objects of perception. Sometimes an image would be green or blue mixed with red. This stimulus was different from the exclusively green and blue signals. The brain began to note the difference between stimulus containing red signals and stimulus without red signals. The correlation of these new signals with specific objects of perception began to forge a new association networks in the brain.

Learning to recognize the "meaning" of these new red signals just is the formation of this new association networks in the color vision processing system. By perceiving a little red in this and a little red in that; and, a lot of red in this and a lot of red in that, each new observation served to strengthen the new associations of the newly emerging red-aware perception network. Eventually, the monkeys developed clusters of neurons able to resonate with a relatively pure form of red wavelength color awareness. This network of neurons could now distinguish between red and non-red. Compare and contrast, "well that's all there is!"

The timing of the behavioral change signaling the

development of new color vision is also revealing. The researchers report new color vision behavior occurred 20 weeks after treatment. This corresponded with what they called "robust levels of transgene expression." Transgene expression is just another way of saying increased numbers of new red cone cells which they measured with photography using light reflected by the red cone cells. In this way, they charted the growth of red cone cells beginning at nine weeks and increasing in both area and density over the following 24 weeks.

The monkeys were tested daily for red-green color vision. These trials included the highly motivating grape juice reward system. In effect, each session was a powerful motivational training exercise. These monkeys really wanted to see color on that screen. One wonders if new color vision would emerge in the same way without these regular motivational training exercises. It would be informative to repeat the study using different levels of motivation. I suspect new color vision, like most adult learning, requires both strong motivation and plenty of experience.

It is likely the brain's ability to process the new red color vision signals was gradual as each new neuron joined the association network that would eventually resonate with red color awareness. The new behavior would only emerge after a critical-mass of associated neurons learned to resonate in this way. This cluster would then form a new category of understanding with neurons in the frontal lobes where volitional behavior begins.

There is a well-known optical illusion which appears to be either a vase or the outline of two faces facing each other. How this is perceived depends upon which cluster of neurons happen to be resonating with awareness during the perceptual experience. The shift between the two ways of understanding the image is usually experienced as abrupt because from a rational perspective the image can not logically be both a vase and two faces at the same time. The perception of the physical matter in the image is either the central vase or the lateral faces. If the vase is the physical material, the faces must be empty space and vice versa. Since matter doesn't pop into and out of existence (except on the quantum level), the contrast between these two mutually exclusive ways of perceiving the image is sharp. We would expect a similar kind of experience with new color perception for the same reason. Red is not green. Once you get it, you get it. When this happens, it's grape juice all the way!

Color perception is just one of the many facets of specialized neural processing making up the vastly complex visual perception system. There are many other specialized clusters of neurons able to resonate with many other types of contextual awareness. Researchers have identified visual processing functions for the perception of color, contrast, motion, position, facial recognition and much more.

Researchers are able to identify the different facets of perceptual processing by noting the symptoms which arise when these functions fail, usually as a result of insult or injury to the system.

There is a visual perception disorder wherein all motion is experienced as a series of abruptly changing static images. A different visual perception disorder presents with blindness to everything except objects in motion. There is a facial recognition disorder characterized by the inability to recognize faces, even the faces of close family members all the while being completely normal in every other way. Each of these specialized functions of visual processing is experienced and expressed through activation of distinct clusters of neurons which have learned to calculate differences and similarities between the signals of the visual data stream within a particular context and so resonate with specialized awareness.

Together, all of these many clusters of specialized visual processing form something like a committee of visual experience. Each member of the visual information processing committee contributes its ongoing interpretation of the raw data stream. The information is made available to associated networks of both specialized and generalized visual processing and then by extension on to other clusters of awareness in the higher level association cortex. It all gets extremely complicated very fast. Each group of specialized neurons contributes its vote on the salience of its awareness. Each of these clusters then adds a voice to the choir of perception generating the qualia of the visual experience.

So here again, perception is another example of the "wisdom of the crowd" and once again statistics models reality and helps us understand and describe the nature of consciousness. The associations between plants in a meadow, colonies of bacteria, colonies of ants, colonies of bees and clusters of neurons inducing specialized awareness are best understood as a process of sampling and calculating of the similarities and differences between the signals of sensation and the catalog of experience.

Suppose you're reading these words while sitting outside. If an eagle were to fly by passing across your peripheral visual field, there would be changes in your visual processing centers. Specialized clusters of neurons sensitive to motion in the periphery would calculate the distance and direction of the newly observed object. The image on the retina of an eagle flying fifty yards away and that of a bee flying inches away have many things in common. The difference in our responses to these two similar but different experiences is due to the many calculations of compare and contrast observations made by specialized clusters in the visual and auditory processing centers. The result is we usually do not swat at the bird.

A similar process to that of visual perception underlies all perceptual experiences. Each of the senses generates a nearly constant stream of data continually sampled and evaluated by many clusters of specialized awareness vying for consideration at the next level of consciousness. Each dedicated group of compare and contrast evaluation neurons performs an assessment of the similarities and differences of the ever-changing signal stream from within its' perceptual context. Auditory, visual, olfactory, gustatory and tactile perceptions all operate in this way, and each of these senses includes many specialized facets of context specific awareness.

Perception is a complex process as seen from just one sensory organ system. The complexity of consciousness increases exponentially as the entire orchestra of sensory signals comes into play. The same principles apply. Each sensory system forms association networks with clusters of context driven neurons which form connections with super-ordinate clusters of awareness eventually coming together to form the association networks bridging sensory modalities providing a meta-awareness of the perceptual experience. The signal streams of sensory systems are continually simultaneously processing and selectively passing on to the next level of consciousness information for further evaluation. Each cluster of awareness emerges through assessing the similarities and differences of context specific perceptions referenced to catalogs of experience. This then is the bubbling cauldron of ever-changing dynamic, transitional and relational signal transfer out of which consciousness emerges.

Up until this point, we have been describing the sensory organ systems signal processing and the perceptions of sensory organ system signal processing operating below the level of normal human waking consciousness. Though the information processing at this level is amazingly beautiful and complex, things get even more interesting with the addition of the conceptions of object-intended thought and the abstractions of language.

Nature 461, 784-787 (8 October 2009) Gene therapy for red–green color blindness in adult primates. Katherine Mancuso, William W. Hauswirth, Qiuhong Li, Thomas B. Connor, James A. Kuchenbecker, Matthew C. Mauck, Jay Neitz & Maureen Neitz

Wiesen, TN, Hubel DH (1963). "Effects of visual deprivation on morphology and physiology of cell in the cat's lateral geniculate body." Journal of Neurophysiology 26 (6): 978–993. PMID 14084170.

9 CONCEPTION AND LANGUAGE

We began with a model of "knowing" based on "compare and contrast," and we have been comparing and contrasting ideas under consideration ever since. It is important to recognize that as we compare and contrast concepts; we are not actually comparing and contrasting the concepts themselves. Instead, we are comparing and contrasting our abstract mental representations of the concepts. Language is the way we juggle abstract mental representations of reality as we try to make sense of the universe.

The difference between a mental representation of a concept and the concept itself is an important distinction because it is here that we have shifted from the concrete world of chemistry and physics to the subjective universe of conception and thought, and with this change, we have introduced many avenues of potential confusion and error.

We learned that communication is the sending and receiving of information which alters consciousness. We also learned the signals of communication can be transmitted directly as chemically coded messages or indirectly as behaviorally coded messages. Language is the behaviorally coded communication defined as a body of words or signs combined with a system for their usage.

So what constitutes a body of words or signs, and what makes up a system of usage? The waggle dance of the honeybee appears to loosely fit this definition. The dance behaviors could be a small body of words or signs, and there is a system for performing the dance on the honeycomb. So is the waggle dance a language? There is a good reason to believe it is not.

For the bee, the dance is not "talking" about the location of nectar. Instead, it is a compressed time reenactment of the flight behaviors leading to the nectar. The reenactment is an outward reflection of the bee's psychological state as the bee recalls the trip. It is not communication about the flight because as far as the bee's nervous system is concerned, it is the flight. So the waggle dance is better understood as an outward expression of the bee's internal state as the bee re-experiences the flight leading to the nectar.

All creatures sufficiently developed so as to have an autonomic nervous system express their internal states of anger, fear and lust through behavior. These expressions make sense because anger, fear, and lust just are the autonomic motivators of behavior. These expressions, like the waggle dance, are outward reflections of the organism's internal state. They are not language. Instead, they are, for lack of a better term, how the organism is feeling rather than what it is saying. They are the reflections of perceptions as the organism directs attention inward.

There is an important distinction between a perception and a thought. Perceptions are always experiential. That is to say; they are not object-directed. In other words, they are not about anything. Rather, they are the feeling or psychological state associated with the act of experiencing. Thoughts, on the other hand, are always about something, real or imagined. Thoughts are object-directed. Language begins with the development of object-intended thought.

So we see a progression in the development of consciousness starting with sensation (sensing), leading to perception (feeling), leading to reflection (behaving) leading to object-intended thought (conception), ultimately leading to the development of interactive rules based associations between object-intended thoughts which is language. The waggle dance is not object-intended and therefore does not qualify as language. It is only with object-intended thought that language begins to have something to talk about.

Language naturally emerges with the development of complex nervous systems operating within social structures. Fish, amphibians, and reptiles are not very social, which is just another way of saying their communications are limited to the outward reflections of their internal states of anger, fear and lust.

Their interactive group behaviors, such as the schooling of fish, are based on instinct and reflex governed by simple stimulus and response circuits. If everybody goes left, go left. If everybody goes right, go right. Stay close. Not too close. Try to be in the middle. There is no evidence of object-intended thought here.

The lack of object-intended thought is why many people feel uncomfortable when interacting with non-social creatures like reptiles. In the absence of object-intended thought, there is no sense of a social connection. Reptiles seem creepy precisely because they have no object-intended social aspect to their consciousness. There is no one "there" with whom to connect.

Social creatures also express their primal autonomic states of anger, fear and lust, but with social animals, we begin to see the expression of bonafide object-intended thought which signals the earliest beginnings of language. It is no coincidence object-intended thought, and complex social structures develop together.

Nature is always seeking ways to stack the deck in favor of survival. Social structures combine with object-intended thought because doing so enhances survival. We see this playing out in the object-intended warning calls of prairie dogs alerting the community to threats. As always, survival is the name of the game.

The prairie dogs' primary defense against predators is running to the safety of the burrow. Professor Con Slobodchikoff of Northern Arizona University has studied prairie dogs for over 30 years. He has looked at the way prairie dogs use warning calls and found they use different warning calls for several different kinds of threats. When a threat comes from above, perhaps a hawk, one particular warning call is sounded. When this is heard, the community looks up. A different call means a fox is on the prowl, and a still different call indicates the presence of a snake. In each case, the community responds by directing attention towards the type of threat indicated.

In experiments evaluating prairie dog calls, humans dressed in identical clothing except for shirt color walked through the prairie dog community four times as warning calls were recorded for later analysis. The pitch of the warning calls varied according to the color of the shirt worn by the intruder. Further analysis showed the warning calls also changed according to the height of the intruder. It was as if the lookout was announcing to the community, "Hey everybody look out, here comes that tall human in the blue shirt again."

A different study in the series revealed that distinct warning calls alerted for the presence of various abstract shapes displayed across the community four feet above the ground using a pulley system. "Look out everybody; here comes the triangle again." It is easy to see how a warning system which specifies the nature of a threat increases survival.

The warning calls of prairie dogs represent object-intended thought. These sounds and gestures become associated with the dog's abstract mental representation of the object intended. The community shares a common set of associations between warning call and type of threat.

Whenever a prairie dog hears a particular call, it is likely the dog experiences the neurological activation pattern corresponding to the memory of the referenced object of intention. This reaction then activates the autonomic fight or flight response to deal with the threat. In this way, the prairie dog responds the warning call in the same way as sensing the threat directly thereby providing a significant survival advantage.

The ScienceNow television program entitled "How Smart Are Animals?" explored object-intended communication across several species. It featured a parrot named Alex, a border collie named Chaser and most impressively, a group of dolphins able to use object-intended thought to plan and execute collaborative group behavior.

The parrot Alex was studied by animal cognition scientist Irene Pepperberg for over thirty years. Alex could verbally identify 50 different objects by name and could distinguish between quantities of up to six objects. He could also distinguish seven colors and five shapes by name and could apply the compare and contrast concepts bigger, smaller, same and different.

Alex also exhibited behaviors consistent with surprise and anger when challenged with nonexistent objects or when "fooled" by objects different from what he had been led to believe was being hidden. He demonstrated these skills with complete strangers suggesting a consciousness beyond rote learning or simple classical conditioning.

With several objects held up in front of the bird, the trainer might ask "which is the green key Alex?" To answer, Alex would reach forward and select the green key with his beak. In a compare and contrast task, the researcher would present two items and then ask a question. For example, a small green metal key might be presented with a big yellow plastic key along with the question "what is the same." The bird would answer "shape." If asked "what is different," the bird would answer "color." If asked "how many," the bird would say "two."

Alex could distinguish between objects based color, shape, and quantity. The mental image of each object in the bird's catalog of experience had become neurologically associated with the object's name sound. When a match between name sound, object-property, and object-memory occurred, the clusters of neurons experiencing the association would then associate with the bird's voluntary motor cortex causing the bird to reach forward and select the appropriate object of intention.

The bird motivation emerged from a neurological "negotiation" between the lower level autonomic drivers of behavior (anger, fear and lust) and the higher level reward system motivators of the forebrain. Motivation was enhanced by a process developed by Dr. Peppercorn called the "model/rival technique" wherein two trainers worked together to demonstrate appropriate responses.

This brief description of some of the neurological events taking place during a simple object selection task barely scratches the surface of the vastly complex information processing taking place during each moment in the life of all conscious creatures. Brains are astonishingly complex, and with the addition of object-intended thought, the complexity of consciousness increases exponentially.

The permutations of conscious states available to the 100 billion neurons in the human brain have been estimated to exceed the total number of subatomic particles in the universe. The ability to cognitively model objects of intention and associate them with name sounds and gestures allows for an infinite number of possible conscious experiences.

Each new name sound and gesture in association with each new object of intention can serve as a new cognitive placeholder for building a new concept or idea. These new ideas can then be strung together to make up the properties of still newer categories of understanding. The possibilities for the creation of new classes is infinite. It is with the development of object-intended thought that the real business of consciousness begins.

Chaser is a Border Collie with the remarkable ability to retrieve over a thousand different toys by name upon request. Psychologists Alliston Reid and John Pilley trained the dog. Chaser's performance on the ScienceNow show was awe-inspiring. After flawlessly retrieving several randomly chosen toys by name from a huge pile of toys on the living room floor, the host performed a seemingly impromptu experiment with the dog.

Ten known toys were selected from the dog's extensive collection and placed in a staging area behind the living room couch together with one new unknown toy named "Darwin." The host appeared to be working with the dog for the first time. He successfully prompted the dog to retrieve several known toys from the staging area. The dog was then asked to "get Darwin," the new unknown toy. The dog immediately went to the staging area and surveyed the available toys. After some hesitation, the dog returned without a toy and looked up at the host. You could almost hear the dog say, "What did you ask for?" The host repeated the command "Get Darwin." The dog then went back to the staging area and seemed to consider each toy carefully. After a few moments, the dog picked up the new unknown toy "Darwin" and delivered it back to the host demonstrating deductive reasoning based on language.

It is easy to imagine how this procedure may have been

used to teach the dog its vast catalog of objects and name sound associations. The dog was obviously highly motivated to play the game. This motivation is an expression of the dog's strong socialization instinct. Strong motivation creates the ideal conditions for the development of new associations in the brain. The grape juice motivated color vision monkeys, the model/rival technique motivated parrot, and now the collie's socialization instinct all suggest the importance of motivation for new learning.

Several processes must occur in the dog's brain to accomplish the "get a novel object" retrieval task. Like the parrot, the dog easily retrieved several known objects by name. The name sounds for each toy matched up with the dog's name sound and object of intention catalog of experience. It is likely these association networks functioned the same way in both the dog and the parrot.

Upon hearing the command "Get Darwin," we see something new. The dog recognizes the game but not the name sound "Darwin." Oh well, worry about that later. The context of the game is sufficient to motivate the dog to go to the staging area and look around. In the staging area, it is reasonable to presume a process of compare and contrast took place, "You're not Darwin, you're fluffy. You're not Darwin; you're Bongo. You're not Darwin; you're Splasher." Each potential solution was assessed by comparing and contrasting the name sound Darwin with the catalog of known objects of intention.

Each item in the dog's mental inventory is functionally equivalent to an association between some cluster of neurons which resonates with awareness upon hearing the name sound and some other group of neurons which stores the associated visual information about the toy. It is likely each of these associations also includes tactile, olfactory, gustatory and emotional connections as well.

Since there was no link between the name sound "Darwin" and any of the other objects of intention in the dog's catalog and since each of the other toys in the staging area already had an association between its name sound and visual memory, the dog's choice emerged through the process of elimination. Darwin was the only object in the group with no previously established name sound and object of intention association. In comparing and contrasting available options, Darwin stood out. As the Sesame Street song put it, "one of these things was not like the others."

This example of compare and contrast processing demonstrates the ability to distinguish between known and unknown toys. Since none of the known toys linked with the name sound "Darwin," and since all the other toys had associations with other name sounds, the unknown toy became the best solution. The ability to distinguish between known and unknown associations is a major step forward in the development of consciousness. It demonstrates awareness of awareness. In effect, the behavior indicates the dog knows what he doesn't know.

A hallmark of intelligence is the ability to plan for the future. Planning requires the mental simulation of behaviors and prediction of potential outcomes. It is easy to see how successful prediction increases survival. The anticipation of problems can save resources and avoid unnecessary dangers.

The final segment of the ScienceNow show featured dolphins with the amazing ability to plan and execute a new team behavior upon request. Researchers from the Marine Mammal Behavior and Cognition Laboratory at the University of Southern Mississippi devised an elegant two-step experiment designed to determine if dolphins can plan behaviors. In the first step of the experiment, the dolphins were taught the concept, "Create a new behavior." Upon learning this concept, individual dolphins would perform something new upon request.

Being asked to do something new means, the dolphins must distinguish between actions previously performed for the trainer and behaviors not previously performed for the trainer. This is similar to the dog distinguishing between known and unknown objects. However, this next step in the mental abstraction of reality requires the dolphin to consider the trainer's perspective. The dolphin must see the trainer's point of view as being different from their own to distinguish between previously demonstrated behaviors and behaviors not previously seen by the trainer.

In the second step of the experiment, the dolphins were taught the concept "perform a behavior together." Upon learning this behavior qualifier, the dolphins would perform known behaviors with other dolphin upon request. With these two abilities established the components of the experiment were set in place.

On film, and in real-time, two of the star dolphins were given the compound command "create" and "together" for the first time. The dolphins were being asked to communicate with each other in such a way as to plan and execute a new coordinated behavior together as a team for the first time.

When the command "create together" was given, both dolphins submerged and interacted in what looked like a conference of gestures, clicks, and whistles. After a few moments, they both swam to the performance staging area, and as a team both dolphins turned over and swam away on their backs while simultaneously lifting their tails up out of the water. The researcher excitedly said, "That's monumental. They've never done that before."

To understand the concept create or "do something

different," the dolphins must be able to keep track of what they've already done suggesting an element of self-awareness. The dolphins must see themselves as different from others to distinguish between previously performed behaviors and previously witnessed or imagined actions. Additionally, in planning a new team behavior, the dolphins needed to formulate a goal-directed future and then bring that future to fruition. It is language which allows for the sequential ordering of abstract conceptions which makes all this possible.

Knowing is the relational association between categories of understanding and learning is the creation of a new association between categories of understanding. When I say "red rubber ball," several categories of understanding are likely to become activated in the listener. You may think something along the lines of, "round red thing that bounces." You might even generate a mental image of a red rubber ball in your mind's eye. Each of these cognitions occurs as distinct clusters of neurons representing different categories of understanding become activated in the brain. This signal transfer between neurons just is the experience of being aware of the combined concept "red round bouncy thing called a ball."

The "round" category includes items like planets, eggs, and eyeballs. The "bounces" category includes balls, tires, checks and undelivered emails. And the red category includes blood, fire engines, and roses. If you deal with red rubber balls on a regular basis, these associations become more firmly established, and so together they form a neural network which takes on the properties of a discrete category of understanding. This is what it means to know something.

The ability to form associations between clusters of neurons abstractly representing objects of intention and neurons representing name sounds occurs in creatures as simple as a parrot selecting green keys upon request. Prairie dogs take communication to the next level with a shared catalog of associations between warning calls and objects of intention allowing them to signal others about specific threats to the community. A strongly motivated border collie can then generate a catalog of over a thousand different name sound and object of intention associations and can even distinguish between the purely abstract categories of "known" and "unknown" objects. And dolphins demonstrate a form of communication which captures almost all of the properties of human language including the ability to plan and perform a goal-directed group behavior suggesting self-awareness.

Self-awareness is an abstraction made up entirely from other abstractions. It is an additional step removed from the "objects of intention" level of awareness. Researchers have devised a simple way to assess for the presence of self-awareness using a mirror and a magic marker. Since most animals do not have self-awareness, most animals respond to their own reflection in a mirror as if seeing another animal. When researchers surreptitiously place an "X" on the face of self-aware animals, however, they react to their reflection very differently. Chimpanzees become immediately curious about the mark and will touch the "X" on their forehead while examining themselves closely in the mirror. You can almost hear them thinking, "what is that mark doing on my forehead?"

In this way, researchers have documented simple self-awareness in elephants, dolphins and the great apes. Keeping in mind what we have learned about communication and consciousness, it makes sense that each of these self-aware species has a rich social life with strong bonds of affiliation along with advanced communication skills. It is with self-awareness that complex social structures become possible.

Communication between self-aware creatures tends to be highly interactive because social animals are strongly motivated to predict, understand and influence the behavior of others. After all, it is the ability to predict, understand and influence others which makes social creatures social. This is an expression of the instinctively motivated socialization drive.

When self-awareness, awareness of other minds, socialization and language combine we see almost all aspects of human consciousness. We are getting very close to what it means to be human. The next step in the development of consciousness for self-aware social creatures with a strong motivation to predict, understand and influence others in the face of competition for limited resources is the emergence of deliberate, intentional strategic deception. When all of these conditions come together, there is a survival based motivation to mislead others. This is the birth of lying.

Most people like to think of nature as honest and pure. It is not. Nature is first and foremost about survival and if deception advances the goal, so much the better. Fraud occurs throughout the natural world. Camouflage is deception. Some non-poisonous snakes take on the bright, vivid colors and general appearance of their poisonous cousins as a deceptive ruse against predators. The angler fish offers a fraudulent lure to unsuspecting prey, and we see deception in the aforementioned tonic immobility reflex. The list goes on.

These forms of deception are naturally selected as each species strives to carve out a niche for survival. With the emergence of self-awareness and the ability to cognitively model the minds of others, we see a new layer in the complexity of consciousness out of which emerges new possibilities for advancing survival. If I know what you know, and if I know what you do not know, I will have a significant advantage as we both compete for the same limited resources.

Researchers have documented intentional deception among the great apes. Chimpanzees will actively conceal things from others and are skillful at manipulating, to their own advantage, whether or not others can see them. In one research paradigm, a low ranking member of the troop is allowed to see a researcher hide a banana. The witness knows going directly for the treat will trigger the intervention of higher ranking members, so he sets out to intentionally misdirect the competition by conspicuously walking to the far end of the enclosure. Once the higher ranking members have been led away by the deceiver's curious behavior, the deceiver sneaks back to eat the banana.

It is only natural to have a negative feeling about deception. Most of us have been adversely affected. We can take some small comfort in recognizing that this natural adaptation is a necessary step in the development of human consciousness. Just as the Cambrian Explosion emerged from the evolutionary pressures of new vision technology, human consciousness expanded due to survival pressures related to language and intentional deception.

It takes a great deal more cognitive processing power to make sense of a complex social environment which now includes subterfuge. Who within the community is a friend and who is not? The fact that rivals often tell the truth while friends sometimes lie complicates the calculation. Under what conditions is deception likely and when can others be trusted? These are the kinds of complex mental calculations upon which survival now depends.

When self-awareness and the awareness of other minds combines with language and intentional deception, we see two significant outcomes. The first is humanity's dominance over the natural world. This dominance occurs because self-awareness, awareness of other minds, language and deception combine to allow for a fluid manipulation of synthetic simulations of reality stacking the deck in favor of desired outcomes. To illustrate the power of these mental fabrications let's do another little thought experiment.

Imagine a yellow canary perched in a tree. Good. Now, down by the water's edge, imagine an alligator sunning himself along the shore. Okay, now imagine a man walking along the trail wearing a blue shirt. Because you have human consciousness, it is likely you can quickly bring these images to mind. It is also likely a prairie dog upon hearing the warning call for a hawk brings the image of a bird to mind.

The leap forward in human consciousness comes with the addition of language and the capacity for deception. So if I now ask you to imagine a blue canary with an alligator's head and human feet walking along the shore, most people can generate a mental image of this absurd creature; a creature which has never existed in the history of the universe except in the mind of man.

In the absence of language, birds, dogs, and apes cannot perform this sort of complex information processing task. They simply do not have the sophisticated conceptual placeholders of language which allows for the fluid manipulation of ideas. Language is the unleashing of human imagination, and it springs forth directly from the pressures of competition, object-intended thought and the ability to lie.

There are many types of specialized neurons in the brain performing many specialized functions inducing many forms of awareness all simultaneously working together. Evidence for these specialized structures comes from deficits seen after insult or injury to specific areas of the brain. For instance, there is an area of the brain where damage reliably results in prosopagnosia or "face blindness."

The ability to recognize and interpret faces offers a significant survival advantage. Quickly identifying who is a friend and who is a foe can mean the difference between life and death. For this reason, humans have an extremely sophisticated facial recognition system. Some are so skilled at facial recognition they can identify celebrities from their baby pictures.

The area of the brain spanning the inferior aspect of the occipital and temporal lobes is called the fusiform gyrus, and it plays a key role in the facial recognition process. Damage to this area can cause face blindness characterized by the inability to recognize even the faces of close family members.

There are many other specialized facets of consciousness in the brain. It is the number of specialized functions and the level of their integration which determines intelligence and ability. The evidence suggests that the neurological association networks of language form many of the structural bridges integrating specialized consciousness functions.

Research on rats shows how the absence of integration between specialized consciousness functions limits the rat's ability to effectively utilize multimodal environmental cues toward achieving a goal (Cheng 1986.) These studies used a rectangular box with food placed in one corner to assess performance. The rat is placed in the center of the box and allowed to note the location of food in the corner. The rat is then removed from the box and caused to be spatially disoriented.

When placed back into the center of the box, it moves directly toward the food about fifty percent of the time. When it fails to go directly toward the food, it tends to go in the opposite direction. This makes sense because from the rat's perspective both the food corner and the diagonally opposite corner have the same spatial orientation as seen from the center of a rectangular box. The environment simply does not have enough information for the rat to know which side of the box contains the food.

If the box is changed to include one blue wall, the environment now has all the information necessary to navigate directly to the food every time. Even with a blue wall, the rat still only gets it right about half the time. Rats can see the difference, but they are unable to use the color information in conjunction with the spatial orientation information. They can not simultaneously process the space concept "far left-hand corner" and color concept "adjacent to the blue wall." Rats lack the specialized neurons bridging the spatial processing and the color processing systems. There is no intra-cluster structure of neurons to parallel process these two different modalities of perception. Rats cannot utilize both spatial and color information at the same time and neither can young human children.

In the absence of language, the developing human brain is unable to effectively integrate both spatial and color awareness at the same time. Like rats, young children rely primarily on the shape of the environment for their orientation. The shape and color processing centers of young children initially function like isolated islands of awareness. Each connects to the more primal structures of the brain, and each communicates with the neocortex, but in the absence of language, these modes of perception are not effectively parallel processed.

Language plays a pivotal role in the development of this parallel processing. Parallel processing of multimodal cues corresponds with the development of language indicating the multimodal processing. A young child might describe an object as being "in the corner" or as being "by the blue wall," but young children do not speak using multimodal language such as, "in the corner by the blue wall" indicating the presence of parallel processing. It is not merely that language signals the ability to parallel process, the evidence suggests the abstractions of language are themselves the neurological bridges doing the parallel processing. Language is the parallel processing.

This is supported by a series of studies using a dual-task paradigm examining the influence of language on multimodal information processing (Hermer-Vazquez, 1999). In the first experiment of the series, the adult subjects were able to reorient themselves using multimodal cues in the absence of a secondary task, however, when engaged in a secondary task of verbally shadowing continuous speech, they were unable to use conjoined multimodal cues for orientation. When their language processing was distracted by verbal shadowing, they could not parallel process multimodal signals.

The failure to parallel process multimodal cues could have resulted from the increased demand on the system brought on by the dual task itself. In a second experiment designed to answer this question, subjects engaged in a non-verbal secondary task shadowing a continuous rhythm were able to reorient themselves in the same way as non-shadowing subjects suggesting the interference in the first study did not result from exceeding the limits of working memory or attention.

In another study in the series, verbally shadowing subjects detected and remembered both geometric and non-geometric information, but were unable to combine these two types of information to specify the position of an object. Taken together, these studies and many others like them indicate the parallel processing of spatial and color information signals depends upon language development.

Human consciousness emerges from the integration of many facets of awareness often parallel processed through language based association networks. The difference between the brain of a rat and the brain of a human is the number of specialized facets of awareness and the level of integration between these neurological structures. Just as the sophistication of communication between social creatures defines their social development, the sophistication of communication between clusters of awareness in a brain defines intellectual development. Human consciousness emerges with the integrations of language based association networks.

So with language we see the development of self-awareness, awareness of other minds, elaborate deception and even the integration of parallel processing allowing for the creation of entirely synthetic mental realities. Each facet of perception can become a new variable in the creation of still newer synthetic realities. All of this unbridled imagination permits the planning and innovation which has led to the human dominance of the natural world. It is language which makes all of this possible.

Thanks to language, We made it out of the food chain! Most of us can look forward to long healthy lives with a low probability of predation. Human dominance over the natural world results directly from self-awareness, awareness of other minds, language, deception and the ability to generate entirely synthetic mental realities. Sadly, another outcome to be explored in the next chapter is the development of mental illness.

Cheng, K. Cognition, 23 (1986) 149-178 A purely geometric module in the rat's spatial representation

Hermer-Vazquez, L, Spelke, E & Katsnelson A. Cognitive Psychology 39, 3–36 (1999) Sources of Flexibility in Human Cognition: Dual-Task Studies of Space and Language.

10 THE ORDER OF EFFECTS OF CONSCIOUSNESS

People enjoy art because art illuminates truth. It does so in some surprising ways. This is because artistic insight tends to emerge from the neurological associations operating below the level of language based processing. Non-language-based neural association networks are more directly connected to "reality" than language based associations because they lack the additional layers of abstraction and ambiguity inherent in language processing. Art is popular precisely because it resonates with these deeper levels of consciousness. In short, Art feels good because art reflects Truth. Arthur C. Clarke's novel and movie, 2001: A Space Odyssey is an example of artistic insight illuminating the effects of dishonesty on mental health.

The story features a sentient computer managing the systems onboard a spacecraft during a long duration flight to Jupiter. In an interview before liftoff, the computer seemed to take great pride in reporting the flawless performance of all HAL 9000 series computers. A pride before the fall because "Hal" was unable to resolve the conflict between his global function to relay information accurately and his mission specific orders to conceal information from the crew.

The first hint of trouble began during a seemingly casual conversation between Hal and crew member Dave Bowman. Dave's suspicions grew when Hal asked him about rumors circulating on the base before liftoff concerning the true purpose of the mission. Dave asked Hal if the question was part of an official psychological evaluation. Hal was then forced to lie in order to continue withholding the mission's secret purpose.

He abruptly changed the subject by reporting a false impending equipment failure warning. When the crew was unable to validate the false report, they lost confidence in the computer and decided to shut down its higher cognitive functions. They made sure the computer could not hear their deliberations, but they failed to realize it could read their lips. Faced with deactivation, Hal concluded the only way to ensure mission success was to kill the entire crew.

Most non-organic mental health problems arise from conflicts between clusters of neurons abstractly representing incongruent versions of reality within the language based processing centers of the brain. That is to say, the dissonance generated by conflicting versions of what is "true" causes the distress experienced as mental illness. To treat these problems most directly is to amend the association networks inducing the incongruent beliefs.

The order of effects of consciousness is a model of consciousness mapping out the level at which neurological processing occurs. Different levels in the order of effect of consciousness correspond to the various structures inducing conscious experiences. Each successive layer in the order of effect of consciousness emerges from the signal transfer patterns between structures experiencing antecedent levels of signal processing. The "Order of Effect" of consciousness describes the level at which signal transfer happens. In other words, the "Order of Effect" of consciousness is a way of tracking just what is aware of what.

The ongoing narrative of everyday human waking consciousness emerges most directly from the signal transfer patterns between neurons located within the language based association cortex of the brain. These signal transfer patterns are induced by the signal transfer patterns of other language and non-language based systems.

Each of these facets of consciousness, in turn, emerges from the signal transfer patterns of still other levels in the order of effect of consciousness. And so it goes. The signal transfer patterns expressed at each level of consciousness induce the succeeding levels of consciousness. Whenever information processing problems occur, understanding the level in the order of effect of consciousness at which the problem arises will suggest the treatment most likely to help.

Hal's psychosis, for example, emerged from contradictions in the logic function of his language based processing. His psychotic behavior was in some ways a reasonable reaction to the situation encountered as he tried to do his job well.

It began with the contradiction between his global function to relate information accurately and his orders to conceal the true purpose of the mission from the crew. The mission was actually intended to investigate radio signals coming from Jupiter proving we are not alone in the universe. The information was kept secrete because it was feared humanity was not ready cope with the news.

As the computer tried to fulfill both mutually exclusive objectives, the increasing instances of deception caused an ever-increasing dissonance and distress forcing the computer to allocate more and more cognitive resources to the growing problem as it tried to calculate a solution for the ever-increasing probability of failure based on the projected outcomes from earlier attempts at maintaining the deception. In a human mind this would be experienced as obsessive and compulsive neurotic thought. When Hal's deceptions finally resulted in the threat of deactivation, the computer concluded the only way to ensure mission success was to kill the crew.

A human seeking help for this kind of problem would

almost certainly receive medications aimed at reducing the symptoms of anxiety, depression, obsessive thought and sleep disturbance. Medication can relieve symptoms, but it does not fix the problem. The order of effects of consciousness allows us to more directly address issues by focusing on the association networks responsible for the distress.

As discussed earlier, there are several ways to alter neurological association networks. The nervous system is constantly changing due to shifts in understanding brought on by new experiences. Since all understanding is dynamic, transitional and relational, even minor changes to one facet of awareness can have significant effects downstream as new information becomes integrated into our fabric of understanding. If we want to get at the distress caused by conflicts within the language based association networks, talk therapy with someone who understands consciousness can be very effective.

Not all psychological problems emerge from conflicts within the language based association network. The defective associations which cause schizophrenia, for instance, occur below the level of language based processing and so talk therapy is not very effective for treating the root cause of this disorder.

Talk therapy can help with the co-occurring situational adjustment problems, but the flawed association networks responsible for the symptoms of schizophrenia itself are simply not rooted in language based processing. The order of effects of consciousness allows us to distinguish between different types of mental illness. To describe the cascading order of effects of consciousness we will start at the sensation level of signal transfer induced consciousness.

To be aware is to be aware of something. For awareness to exist there must be "something" for consciousness to be aware of. Therefore, the first level in the order of effect of conscious experience is any stimulus able to induce awareness. Remember, consciousness emerges from the dynamic, transitional and relational signal transfer patterns of networked structures within a subject as that subject experiences some object or event, real or imagined.

We can conclude that signal transfer patterns between dynamically networked structures induce consciousness in the same way we conclude anything else. The philosopher David Hume described causation as the habit of the mind applied to constantly conjoined events. The stock example of this is a billiard ball striking another billiard ball. The motion of the second ball is said to be caused by the action of the first.

We infer consciousness emerges from dynamically networked signal transfer patterns between neurons because there is a constant conjunction between consciousness and dynamically networked signal transfer patterns between neurons. Every instance of consciousness occurs with dynamically networked signal transfer, and all evidence for consciousness ceases whenever these signal transmission patterns cease.

Now for something to be detectable it must have contrast from its background. There must be a difference between the signals inducing awareness of the stimulus and the signals of everything else (compare and contrast, well that is all there is.) Also, since consciousness is always dynamic, there must be a relational interplay between stimulus signals and the signals indicating everything else.

It is the dynamic interaction of signals contrasting stimulus from non-stimulus which forms the relational matrix of association out of which first order of effect of consciousness emerges. Said another way, the first order of effect of consciousness arises from the dynamically networked signal patterns distinguishing stimulus from everything else. In simplest terms, the first order of effect of consciousness is reality expressing itself.

Any detectable object or event, real or imagined, by virtue of its "detectability" is an expression of signal transfer induced first order of effect consciousness. It is dynamic, transitional and relational signal transfer which induces all conscious experience.

It may seem magical to say dynamic, transitional and relational signal transfer produces consciousness but this is no more mysterious than other well-accepted phenomena in nature. Electromagnetism, for example, is the force expressed whenever the flow of electrons induces a magnetic field. These magnetic fields can then be used to transform electrical energy into the spinning motion of an electric motor. The same force, applied in the opposite direction, allows the physical movement of magnets within a generator to induce the flow of electrons.

Both electromagnetism and consciousness emerge as one type of action induces a new phenomenon with properties completely different from the inducing cause. We get hung up on consciousness and not electromagnetism because with electromagnetism we can measure both the cause and the effect, but with consciousness, we can only measure the signal transfer patterns which induce it. We have no way to measure the consciousness itself except through behavior. Behavior just is the measured effect of consciousness. Let that sink in.

So the first order of effect of consciousness is any detectable stimulus expressing a signal transfer pattern able to induce consciousness. With the consciousness ball now in play, so to speak, nature can associate and compound these instances of signal transfer to produce succeeding expressions of dynamic, transitional and relational signal transfer inducing subsequent layers of consciousness. The order of effect model of consciousness describes the hierarchy of signal transfer patterns inducing consciousness within a system.

With the first level in the order of effect of consciousness being the signal transfer patterns associated with a detectable stimulus, the second level in the order of effect of consciousness is the signal detection process we call sensation. Even a virus exhibits a second level order of effect consciousness as it reacts to the signals indicating the existence of a host cell. It is second tier sensation consciousness which enables the virus to attach itself to the host facilitating infection. Sensation consciousness emerges from the dynamic, transitional and relational signal transfer patterns of an entity as it senses first level order of effect consciousness. To illustrate just how the process works, let's consider a simple mechanical analog of sensation consciousness.

Mechanical thermostats express a second level order of effect consciousness of temperature. Temperature is the energy level of the material being measured. Air conditioner thermostats measure the temperature of room air.

Room air is made up of gas molecules energetically zipping around, slamming into and bouncing off everything in the environment. Change in air temperature is the change in the kinetic energy of these gas molecules. Increased temperature means increased kinetic energy which means more frequent and more powerful collisions between air molecules and the environment. Room temperature just is the measured effect of these collisions.

Metals expand as temperature increases because the atoms making up the metal vibrate more energetically causing them to push further apart from one another. If the temperature gets high enough, the bonds between metal atoms release and the metal will melt into the liquid state. Air conditioner thermostats take advantage of the way different metals expand and contract at different rates as temperature changes.

The second level order of effect consciousness of a thermostat emerges most directly from the dynamic, transitional and relational signal transfer pattern between the two dissimilar metals bonded (networked) together. Because the two metal strips expand and contract at different rates, temperature change causes the bimetal strip to bend. The bending behavior in response to the temperature change just is the behavioral evidence of awareness of changing temperature. As the strip bends, it is made to tilt a gravity dependent switch which then causes the air conditioner to turn on or off.

In this example, the changing kinetic energy of gas molecules represents the first level in the order of effect of consciousness. The dynamic, transitional and relational signal transfer pattern expressed as the bending bimetal strip in response to temperature change is the second level in the order of effect of consciousness.

For creatures with sensory organ systems, the second level in the order of effect of consciousness emerges most directly from the dynamic, transitional and relational signal transfer patterns of sensory receptor cells in the sensory organ detector array as it responds to the signal transfer patterns of first level order of effect consciousness.

There is always a relational aspect to consciousness. In a human eye, for instance, each of the 126 million rods and cones making up each retina's sensory array contributes a "voice" to the choir of retina sensation as the array responds to light. The combined signals of the array generate a signal transfer pattern experienced by the array itself as a second level order of effect consciousness of the first level photons emitted by or reflected off the object being sensed.

Second level sensation consciousness emerges most directly from the dynamic, transitional and relational signal transfer pattern of the array correlating with the spatial, temporal and wavelength properties of the light depolarizing receptor cells. And so the retina itself experiences what could be called "retina consciousness." Sensation is best described as a form of consciousness because, like all consciousness, it emerges from the dynamic, transitional and relational signal transfer patterns of associated structures.

We can better appreciate the nature of emergent consciousness by considering the properties of a high definition television system. A 1080p screen has about two million pixels. Each pixel in the array is a tiny dot of colored light made up of different levels of red, green and blue light. Individual pixels alone do not convey much information, but groups of associated pixels together allow for the emergence of an image. When emergent images are then dynamically transitioned and related to each other, we see the emergence of a dynamic, transitional and relational reflection of reality. The reflection of reality expressed by the screen is a third level response to the first level photons striking the camera's second level sensor array.

When the signals of human visual sensation are transmitted by the optic nerves to neurons in the occipital lobes of the brain, the dynamic, transitional and relational signals induce the third level order of effect of consciousness which we call perception. Perception is the third level in the order of effect of consciousness because perception is the awareness (third level) of sensation (second level) of a stimulus (first level).

Perception is usually thought of as a bottom-up form of signal processing, but the signals inducing perception are actually bottom-up, lateral and top-down signal transfer process. The bottom-up aspect of visual perception occurs as the signals generated by the retina get processed by clusters of neurons in the primary visual cortex. In a similar way, the bottom-up aspect of auditory perception occurs as signals produced by the ear are experienced by neurons in the primary auditory cortex just as the bottom-up aspect of tactile perception occur as receptor cells in the tissues transmit their signals to the somatosensory cortex of the parietal lobes. The more primal chemical signals of scent and taste are initially processed below the level of the neocortex and so these perceptions induce a more system-wide global perceptual experience.

The lateral aspect of third level perception consciousness occurs as other sensory organ systems contribute their signal patterns to the perceptual experience. The brain is extensively integrated. So each perception is "flavored" by all salient modes of sensation including visual, auditory, gustatory, olfactory, tactile as well as the associations of memory and emotion.

The top-down aspect of perception occurs as higher levels in the order of effect of consciousness alter the data stream by applying filters and signal translators making the data more intelligible for the task at hand. For example, a coin seen on the floor from across the room will be perceived as round even though the light striking the retina is elliptical due to the angle of observation. This translation algorithm is applied to the visual data stream because coins are known to be round.

So perception is a third level order of effect consciousness which emerges from the combined signal transfer patterns of multi-modal sensation, emotion, and memory. Together these signal transfer patterns combine to give perception the emergent property we call "qualia."

Qualia is the emergent experiential "feeling" associated with the combined dynamic, transitional and relational signal transfer process of stimulus, sensation, and perception in association with memory and emotion. It emerges from the totality of the signal transfer experience induced by the multi-modal bottom-up, lateral and top-down signal processing experience. It is the combined visual, auditory, gustatory, tactile and olfactory sensations in concert with memory and emotion which gives perception its qualia effect. The "taste of adventure" and "the warmth of a smile" are examples of language pointing to the multi-modal aspect of qualia.

All perceptions are subjective. As such, each percipient has ultimate authority over the nature of their own perceptual experience. Perception is not subject to third-party correction. Because there is no objective measure for the qualia of experience, perception resists scientific investigation. This lack of an objective measure is exactly why the first ten chapters of this book were necessary. It is only through a global understanding of consciousness that we can begin to make reasonable inferences about the properties of perception and the nature of qualia.

The qualia of perception emerges from the totality of the combined multi-faceted signal transfer pattern of stimulus, sensation, memory, imagination, and emotion. Each facet of the experience emerges from the signal transfer patterns of the many different clusters having the experience. The relative strength of each contributing cluster is modulated through habituation and sensitization allowing different aspects of the perceptual experience to be emphasized or downplayed thereby altering the qualia of the experience. This is how subjective perceptions can be modified. In effect, we can choose the qualia of our own experience as evidenced by the development of an "acquired taste." The ability to alter the qualia of an experience in adaptive ways is a good measure of mental health.

The first three levels in the order of effect of consciousness, stimulus, sensation, and perception, combine to form the dynamic transitional and relational signal transfer patterns out of which all subsequent levels in the order of effect of consciousness emerge. Together, stimulus, sensation, and perception set the stage for the survival based arms race of emergent intelligence we call evolution.

Because of the complexity of even the simplest nervous systems, when describing higher levels in the order of effect of consciousness, we run into the same kind of problem faced by weathermen trying to make long-term weather predictions. There are just too many constantly changing variables to make accurate long-term weather forecasts possible. Both global weather patterns and higher levels in the order of effect of consciousness are too complex to be measured directly. There is no practical way to capture and process all the data. Even so, weather predictions based on models and samples of data allow for useful planning, just as understanding the order of effects of consciousness combined with samples of behavior allows us to gauge the conditions likely to promote mental health.

Though I will discuss the higher levels in the order of effect of consciousness as if they exist in discrete form, they do not. All consciousness by its very nature is dynamic, transitional and relational; therefore all consciousness is associated with all other consciousness. Because consciousness is never discrete, the distinctions between the levels in the order of effect of consciousness are offered only as a conceptual aid for understanding a very complicated process.

The fourth level in the order of effect of consciousness is called "reflection consciousness." Reflection consciousness provides the first outward evidence for the presence of consciousness. The movement of bacteria towards sustenance and the growing of plants towards the light are examples of fourth level order of effect reflection consciousness. For more developed organisms, reflection consciousness emerges most directly from the signal transfer patterns between neurons experiencing third level perception consciousness acting in concert with the motor sequences of reflex or instinctive behavior.

Since third level perception consciousness emerges primarily from the signal patterns of second level sensation, and since second level sensation arises most directly from the signal patterns of first level stimulus, reflection consciousness is the nearly instantaneous cascading signal transfer stream of stimulus, sensation and perception in association with motor responses. The waggle dance of the honeybee and the nest building of reptiles are also examples of fourth level order of effect reflection consciousness.

As nervous systems grow in complexity and new specialized structures and functions develop, fourth level reflection consciousness transitions into a fifth level order of effect "abstraction consciousness." An example of fifth level order of effect abstraction consciousness was described earlier as the signal transfer filters and translation algorithms applied to the perceptual data stream making perception more intelligible for the task at hand. This explained why a coin viewed on the floor from across the room is seen as round even though the image striking the retina is elliptical due to the angle of observation. This round abstraction of the retina's elliptical signal allows the organism to model the universe more accurately. The awareness of roundness is a fifth level abstraction of the third level perception.

In addition to data filters and signal translation algorithms, the fifth level in the order of effect consciousness extends the clustering of association cortex networks to induce signal transfer patterns able to resonate with awareness of abstract constructs such as the name of an object or the properties of a category. The fifth level in the order effect of consciousness is the awareness (abstraction) of the awareness (reflection) of the awareness (perception) of the awareness (sensation) of reality (stimulus).

The warning calls of prairie dogs are also an example of fifth level order of effect abstraction consciousness. This consciousness emerges most directly from associations between clusters of neurons inducing awareness of the warning call associated with neurons producing awareness of the memory of a predator in conjunction with the activation of the autonomic fight or flight response. As far as the prairie dog's consciousness is concerned, warning call equals abstract representation of predator which equals fight or flight response. The abstraction level allows the prairie dog to respond to the warning calls with the same urgency as if sensing the predator directly.

The abstraction level of consciousness also allows for the development of cooperative social structures and marks the earliest beginnings of something like language. Most of our daily experiences play out at the fifth level in the order of effects of consciousness. This abstraction level of consciousness tends to be automatic and preconditioned. It is the state of "mind" experienced during routine activities such as driving a car or riding a bicycle.

Driving is usually experienced automatically in a preconditioned sort of way. For experienced drivers changing the car's direction just equals turning the steering wheel, and stopping or slowing down just equals pushing on the brake. There is no "conscious" thought involved. Routine driving can be so automatic people often report having no memory of a routine drive home.

The first five levels in the order of effect of consciousness are experienced "subconsciously" where subconscious is just another way of saying below the level of language based processing. The abstraction level of consciousness notes the constant conjunction between stimulus and response and calculates theories of causation. This is the process we call classical conditioning. Problems at the fifth level in the order of effect of consciousness are responsible for the symptoms of schizophrenia, autism and some organic forms of anxiety and depression.

Each level in the order of effects of consciousness is a distilled sample of the inducing signal data stream. It is an abbreviated interpretation of antecedent levels of consciousness. Each level in the process samples the inducing data stream and captures only the most salient information necessary for efficiently advancing awareness to the next level for the purpose of survival. This distillation process imposes order on an otherwise unmanageable and overwhelming flood of information. The phi phenomenon is an optical illusion allowing us to see how the nervous system samples data to make sense of the universe.

Two lights viewed within the same visual field can be made to flash on and off intermittently in such a way as to produce the illusion of a single light moving back and forth in a pendulum fashion. This illusion occurs at the fifth level in the order of effect of consciousness. It is an abstraction of the lower level consciousness which infers the motion from the sampled data stream. This fifth level of consciousness causes the observer to see a pendulum motion where there is none. The observed pendulum effect emerges as the system applies the constant conjunction rules of moving objects based on the memory of earlier pendulum experiences.

The faulty perceptions of schizophrenia occur at the fifth level in the order of effect of consciousness. This fifth level flaw is why schizophrenia is so resistant to talk therapy. The neurological association networks responsible for generating the false attributions of the schizophrenic emerge from the same abstraction level as the phi phenomenon.

The paranoid delusions of the schizophrenic can seem as real to the sufferer as the illusion of motion perceived in the phi phenomenon. Treating schizophrenia with talk therapy is like asking the patient to believe the therapist's description of reality over their own direct perceptions. Which would you believe?

Conception is the sixth level in the order of effect of consciousness. It is what most people think of when they think about what it means to think. Conception consciousness extends the clustering and compounding of lower and lateral levels in the order of effect of consciousness to induce the signal transfer patterns able to juggle the abstractions of fifth level order of effect consciousness.

Sixth level order of effect of consciousness allows for the application of context driven rules of association between concepts and categories making syntax and language possible. It is only with the development of the sixth level in the order of effect of consciousness that anything like human consciousness comes into being. The sixth level in the order of effects of consciousness is the awareness (conception) of the awareness (abstraction) of the awareness (reflection) of the awareness (perception) of the awareness (sensation) of reality (stimulus). Six steps removed from reality.

It is with the conception consciousness that we generate the complex simulations of reality making imagination and long-term planning possible. This occurs primarily through language based association networks. It is with language that we fabricate a self-concept and project that self-concept through imagined time to replay past events or imagine future possibilities. Most nonorganic mental health problems such as anxiety, depression, obsession and compulsion emerge from conflicted associations within sixth level order of effect of consciousness.

So we see each level in the order of effect of consciousness represents an additional layer of signal processing complexity and an additional layer of subsequent emergent awareness. There is nothing, other than vanity, to suggest that any particular level in the order of effect of consciousness is any more conscious than any other level. The first level order of effect of a ringing bell is in some ways just as conscious as the sixth level order of effect conception of a bell being rung. The idea that a conception is more conscious than a sensation is like believing a meadow is prettier than a flower.

Most people spend their day actively processing their sixth level order of effect conceptions of a reality. Many get stuck in these mental simulations. It is a subtle form of insanity at least six steps removed from actual reality. This entire book has been an exercise using sixth level order of effect language based processing to "conceptually" tunnel down into and then back out of again each of the different levels in the order of effect of consciousness. If you now understand consciousness to be the emergent process of dynamic, transitional and relational signal transfer with cascading orders of effect, you have begun to glimpse a seventh level in the order of effect of consciousness. This is the awareness of your consciousness awaking to the nature of consciousness. Taken to its logical extreme, it is much more than that. It is an awakening to the true nature of consciousness, the universe, and everything because from this seventh level in the order of effect of consciousness we can begin to make our way out of the labyrinth.

11 THE CAULDRON

It is widely believed humans use only ten percent of the brain and can think only one thought at a time. Nothing could be further from the truth. The entire brain is always "on the air" processing countless facets of dynamic, transitional and relational signal transfer all of the time. It has hair-trigger sensitivity and continually fires off signals in response to the flood of messages from both within and outside the system. Even at rest, the brain is like a boiling cauldron of countless separate yet associated facets of signal transfer induced consciousness. There is always much more going on than meets the eye.

We "consciously" experience only those aspects of thought which break the surface of the metaphorical cauldron thereby making it into our overt conscious awareness. These expressions emerge most directly from our language based association networks.

What most people think of as consciousness is just the thin surface layer of a vast deeply textured highly interactive signal transfer process. The language based veneer of consciousness is the story we tell ourselves about ourselves. It is what most people think of as reality, but reality is much more than our language based processing.

Whenever a facet of consciousness is induced by a cascading signal transfer pattern between neurons, all neurologically associated aspects of that consciousness come a little closer to the surface thereby becoming more readily available for processing.

For instance, if I were to ask you the color of your first bicycle, assuming you had one, it is likely you would experience the memory of your first bicycle. In addition, all memories associated with this memory would also become more readily available for processing.

That the system works in this way is well-supported by literally thousands of studies using many different paradigms including studies comparing latency time for the recall of associated versus unassociated memories. Associated memories take less time to access than non-associated memories. This occurs because nervous tissue is excitable. Whenever a neuron is activated, all connected neurons tend to have their action potentials altered thereby increasing their readiness to also be activated. We see evidence for this in Freudian slips, intuition and artistic insight.

We can learn more about the nature of human consciousness by considering the physical layout of the brain itself. There is symmetry between the hemispheres which mirror each other in form and function for both motor control and tactile sensation. The left hemisphere controls to the right side of the body and the right hemisphere controls to the left side of the body. Visual and auditory processing are also crisscrossed and mirrored.

This crisscrossed and mirrored symmetry of sight, sound and touch enhances the integration of the organism with the environment. As the right hemisphere "looks" to the left, it simultaneously monitors both the left side of the body and the left hemisphere's reports about the right-side of the body. In the same way, the left hemisphere oversees the right-side of the body and the right hemisphere's reports about the left-side of the body. Crisscrossed and mirrored command and control enhances the compare and contrast processing of sensory and motor signal for better coordination and interaction with the environment.

Higher level language based processing, on the other hand, is asymmetric. Wernicke's area for speech recognition and Broca's area for speech production are both usually located in the left hemisphere. Asymmetric language processing makes sense because language, in contrast to sight, sound, and touch, does not "connect" directly to the physical universe. Instead, language represents a "reflection" of a "reflection" of the environment. Because there is no direct relationship between the neurological association networks of language and the physical universe to which the language refers, there is no benefit to a mirrored symmetry.

Though our language usually gets processed in the left hemisphere, the right hemisphere also has an understanding of the concepts under consideration during language processing. It comprehends the rudiments of language but tends to experience these cognitions more as feeling and images rather than words and syntax. Without syntax and other nuances of language, the right hemisphere tends to be more literal. For this reason, hypnotic suggestions hoping to enlist both hemispheres ought to be simple and clearly stated. Double negatives, sarcasm, and metaphor do not translate well to the right hemisphere.

Language is the application of abstraction and syntax to represent concepts under consideration. It is an additional abstraction step removed from lower level non-linguistic processing. As such, language tends to be more abstract and more subjective than other lower level processing.

Remember, language developed to model reality to better predict the outcomes of potential actions and events. These language simulations of the past and future tend to play out in the left hemisphere while the right hemisphere tends to process more real-time here and now experiences. Split brain research reveals some interesting findings on differences between the hemispheres.

The term Split-brain is used to describe patients who undergo surgery severing the corpus callosum, a structure of about 250 million nerve fibers connecting and integrating the two hemispheres of the brain. This surgery is usually preformed as a last ditch effort to treat severe seizures.

Seizures are the neurological equivalent to a fibrillating heart which can cause brain damage. Severing the corpus callosum reduces seizures by preventing their spread across the hemispheres. Also, because nervous tissue is naturally excitable, any reduction in the overall volume of signal transfer will also tend to reduce seizures. Most people are surprised to learn patients who undergo this seemingly radical procedure usually appear to be completely normal. Researchers have devised some clever ways to assess the subtle changes which do exist.

Psychologist Michael Gazzaniga has studied split-brain patients for over fifty years. In one research paradigm, Gazzaniga flashed different images to the left and right visual fields at the same time as the subject focused on the center of a display screen. Because the left visual field of both eyes communicates primarily with the right occipital lobe and the right visual field of both eyes communicates primarily with the left occipital lobe, each hemisphere will see a different image. Usually, the corpus callosum allows the hemispheres to share visual information, but after the surgery, there is no direct communication between the hemispheres.

A subject might have the image of grapes flashed to the left visual field while the image of a car flashes to the right. Because the optic nerve crisscrosses back from the eyes to the occipital lobes, the left occipital lobe sees the car in the right visual field while the right occipital lobe sees the grapes in the left visual field. Because language is usually processed in the left hemisphere, when asked, subjects will reliably report seeing a car.

Here is where it gets interesting. Remember, the right-side of the brain which controls the left side of the body saw grapes. If the subject is then asked to close their eyes and draw a picture of the image seen with their left hand, the subject will reliably draw grapes. This is because the right hemisphere saw grapes, and the right hemisphere also controls the left-hand drawing the image. If asked why they drew grapes while reporting seeing a car, they tend to say "I don't know."

It is fascinating to watch a subject peeking down at their own left-hand drawing as their left hemisphere tries to guess what their right hemisphere is trying to say. And so we see each side of the brain experiences distinct simultaneous consciousness.

Other differences between hemispheres is seen in studies looking at the effects of unihemispheric anesthesia on perceptions of self versus other (Keenan et al., 2001). Subjects receiving anesthesia to their individual hemispheres were shown a custom image designed to assess differences in the perception of self versus other.

Researchers created the target images used in the study by combining two photographs with a simple computer morphing program. Each custom image was made by combining the subject's picture with the photo of a well-known public figure to create a target image with characteristics of both the subject and the public figure.

Facial recognition is a complex information processing task performed by specialized clusters of neurons able to compare and contrast subtle differences in the light reflected by the contours of a face. Some people are so skilled at this they can identify adults from baby pictures. When the image of a famous person is combined with the picture of an unknown person, the reliable outcome is easy recognition of the famous person. This is because the specialized clusters of neurons responsible for facial recognition tend to select the best match based on a catalog of known faces. So facial recognition is a fifth level order of effect projection of identification onto the third level perception of an image. It emerges from the compare and contrast calculations of neurons in the facial recognition processing centers of the brain and the memory catalog of known faces.

Patients considered for brain surgery often receive preoperative evaluations to determine the dominant hemisphere for speech and memory. About five percent of right-handed people and about twenty percent of left-handed people have right hemisphere language dominance. Physicians check by anesthetizing each hemisphere individually while assessing language performance.

Before the study, each subject had a custom image created by combining their own image with the image of a well-known public figure. When subjects viewed the target image under left hemisphere anesthesia, they later recalled seeing themselves in the picture. In contrast, when subjects saw the image during right hemisphere anesthesia, they later recalled seeing the well-known public figure in the very same image.

Because subjects did not see themselves in the absence of a functioning right hemisphere, the researchers concluded some critical component of self-awareness must reside in the right hemisphere. Perhaps there is a better explanation.

Why would nature generate a different perception of the same face by different hemispheres of the same brain? Perhaps this asymmetry is related to other asymmetries. Remember language developed to allow for complex, out of time, simulations of reality for predicting outcomes to increase survival. The experience of language is, therefore, something of an altered state of consciousness dissociated from the more direct here and now unfolding of reality. This potentially dangerous state of distraction by the left hemisphere is balanced by the right hemisphere's more direct connection with real-time events. Just as sea mammals exhibit unihemispheric sleep to stay connected to real-time threats, humans may have developed asymmetric language for the very same reason. It just makes sense nature would use the same strategy to compensate for similar states of dissociation.

The language based left hemisphere, therefore, tends to be removed from here and now real-time events as it strives to understand the past and predict the future. This dissociation from the here and now is especially important in social situations where the left brain acts as a strategic assessment and planning machine. It actively reviews the past and imagines the future while the non-linguistic right hemisphere stays more attuned to the here and now events of physical reality.

The left hemisphere tends to be on the lookout for others of importance as it calculates potential risks or benefits of the social world while the right hemisphere tends to stay focused more on the here and now experience of being. So it makes sense the most salient feature of an image during left hemisphere recognition will tend to be others of importance, while the most prominent feature of right hemisphere processing will tend to be the "self" having the here and now experience.

The identification of self is consistent with self-consciousness, but it is misleading to suggest self-identification alone presupposes a full access to one's thoughts and mental states. The narrative of language based consciousness usually unfolds in the left hemisphere, and the selective hemisphere anesthesia studies suggest a component of self-identification resides in the right hemisphere. Rather than supposing a particular group of neurons within the right hemisphere generates the experience of self, it may be that in the absence of the left hemisphere's synthetic out of time abstractions of reality, the distinction between "self" and "other" simply drops out.

"Self-concept" is an abstraction very different from the experience of self. A self-concept might include author, honest, insightful, happy, attractive and productive (hey, it is my book) but none of these abstractions represent the real-time self. These ideas of self only exist as an abstract construct in the language based processing centers of the brain and language based processing is by definition removed from current reality. As soon as you begin to think "self," you are no longer having a self-experience of being. Instead, you are experiencing an abstract representation of the idea of self which is not the self at all.

Also, because of the transitional nature of all consciousness, there can never be distinct self-consciousness completely separate and apart from other consciousness. Self-consciousness like all consciousness is dynamic, transitional and relational. The idea of a separate self somehow apart from the rest of the universe is only an illusion fabricated by the language based processing centers of the brain. Self always relates to other because there is no such thing as a one-sided coin. It is language based processing which manufactures this illusion of a separate self. Furthermore, evidence suggesting this manufactured illusion of self is responsible for almost all human suffering.

In her book, "My Stroke of Insight (2008)", neuroanatomist Dr. Jill Bolte Taylor describes an experience which aligns nicely with the broader point I hope to make about the relationship between language, self-concept, and mental health. Namely, that most non-organic mental illness emerges from a language based fabrication of a separate "self" operating from within a conjured simulation of reality.

Doctor Taylor describes having stroke during which her language based processing was intermittently taken "off-line." In the absence of language, she saw her hand as a beautifully weird claw-like structure. This unusual perception emerged from her inability to associate the image of her hand with her language based abstractions about hands. In the absence of these projections, the hand lost some of its subjective human properties and took on the more objective animal like claw appearance.

Many language based associations facilitate social cohesion by distinguishing human from non-human. This distinction is why most people easily eat chicken wings while few would readily eat real lady fingers. In the absence of language based associations, the hand took the more objective animal claw-like appearance.

She reports shifting back and forth between a right hemisphere non-language based selfless state of "nirvana," free from the anxiety and worries of the world, to a panic-stricken state of alarm generated by her left hemisphere's language based story about her unfolding medical emergency.

She describes the qualia of these two experiences as alternating between a peaceful, expansive blurring of the boundary between self and the universe (right hemisphere) and the overload of pain and fear generated by her language based left hemisphere. The very same event was experienced in two dramatically different ways depending on which clusters of neurons happen to be running the show. The agony of language based consciousness or the bliss of non-language-based consciousness. She found the experience so moving she wrote a book to share about the blissful state of "oneness" available to us all.

It is easy to be skeptical about a non-language-based blissful state of "oneness" as being some sort of new-age bubble headed disconnection from reality. This skepticism results from our tendency to rigidly identify with our language based processing. It is the essence of "ego."

In light of what we have learned about the nature of consciousness, however, we must conclude that language based processing is the real disconnection from reality. The evidenced based nature of consciousness suggests the blissful state described by Doctor Taylor is, in fact, more directly connected to reality than any language based simulation could possibly be. At best, language reflects only a facet of a context driven synthetic reality. The universe is always much more than any language based simulation could possibly conjure.

As far as the brain is concerned, there is no difference between the neurological associations created out of a third level order of effect perception directly reflecting the physical universe and the associations arising out of the imagined sixth level order of effect conceptions of language. That some imagined "realities" accurately predict and reflect reality while others do not, makes no difference to the neural structures having the experience. The brain treats each association in the same way.

Before the integration of language into consciousness there was no disadvantage to strategic deception. When a chimpanzee intentionally misdirects a competitor about the location of a hidden banana, the chimpanzees mental health doesn't suffer. The chimpanzee will not get lost in its own language based simulations of reality manufacturing the fear of retaliation, the self-loathing of moral failings or the anxiety of an impending wrath from a vengeful God.

Earlier we noted how rats lacked the integration between clusters of neurons necessary for combining multimodal cues like "far left-hand corner" and "adjacent to the blue wall." Because human consciousness is extensively interwoven with language based associations, when told the food is in the far left-hand corner adjacent to the blue wall, if the information is accurate, we quickly find the food. If on the other hand, the information is wrong, we tend to generate a language based simulation of reality hoping to come to terms with the discrepancy.

Perhaps the information was misunderstood. Maybe the error was a simple mistake, or maybe it was intentional. Someone else may have moved the food. What previous experience sheds light on the truth? How does this affect other information from the same or similar sources? With the development of self-awareness, awareness of other minds, language and intentional deception there is much more to be considered.

The effectiveness of language for modeling reality depends upon its accuracy. It requires honest, rational, and congruent appraisals of experience. Experiences which include dishonesty and deception tend to create snags in the fabric of our neurological association networks which then conflict with other perceptions of reality. These conflicts can then cause psychological distress experienced as both mental and physical illness.

Those with alcoholism and addiction also suffer from maladaptive incongruent language based versions of reality. Their "truths" become so twisted that their obsessive thoughts and compulsive behaviors are seen as reasonable and appropriate when viewed from within their distorted belief systems. "You would drink too if you had my problems." This sometimes subtle, all too often deadly form of mental illness arises directly from maladaptive association networks in the brain. Removing the additive substance is not a cure. The belief systems must also be amended. Recovery from addiction almost always requires ongoing support to develop and maintain the neurological association networks reflecting a new way of life.

There are many sub-clinical variants of this type of dysfunction. Most human cruelty emerges from conflicted language based neurological association networks generating psychological distress wrongly attributed to the actions of others. The sufferer then blames others for their own discomfort and retaliates against the illusion of threat fabricated by the incongruencies of their own language based processing.

Prejudice and discrimination also emerge from these maladaptive neurological networks causing the over generalization of groups and individuals. Even the brutality of poverty gets justified through the faulty incongruent belief systems of language. Who among us really believes a low-income earner deserves to suffer and die from an easily treated illness just because they lack the funds to pay for simple health care? Only a conflicted mind justifies this kind of dehumanization of others. Telling someone to "get a job" is not only unkind; it tends to further damage the mind of the person making the suggestion.

Perhaps the most pernicious maladaptive beliefs emerge from the contradictions and incongruencies many hold about the nature of reality itself. The belief in a separate "self" somehow apart from the rest of the universe generates a persistent and pervasive dissonance responsible for the clash of cultures, religions, political parties, criminal gangs, sports fans and the list goes on. Wherever there is a conflict you will find at least one, and more often two combatants who have become rigidly identified with the illusion of a separate self under threat. Their language based synthetic "realities" see violence as the most reasonable response to their ego-based fears. These fears are the primary obstacle to happiness and prosperity.

Now that we understand the nature of consciousness we are in a much better position to make rational choices. Our options for responding to unsatisfying consciousness become more clear. Whenever consciousness is found to be unsatisfying, there are only three options. These are the same three options pioneered by the chemotaxis of bacteria. These responses to challenge have been around a long, long time so we can be confident we are on the right track as we consider how best to respond.

The first potential response to the challenge of unsatisfying consciousness is to do nothing at all. This choice usually means suffering with the anxiety of an unrequited desire for a different state of consciousness. It is sometimes a good option because sometimes waiting for more information or a better circumstance resolves the problem. This is equivalent to nature's tonic immobility response.

Another potential response to the problem of unsatisfying consciousness is to reduce consciousness. There are many ways to reduce consciousness such as watching television, shopping, sleeping, taking drugs, drinking alcohol, eating, gambling, the list goes on. These behaviors may or may not be adaptive depending on the circumstance, but if the subject is trying to escape unsatisfying consciousness by reducing consciousness, it is often maladaptive. This is the flight response.

The only other response to unsatisfying consciousness is to increase consciousness. Increasing awareness begins when we direct our attention to the unsatisfying consciousness itself. It is not mounting of an attack on the persons or events associated with the unsatisfying experience; instead, it is action aimed at the root cause of the problem, the unsatisfying consciousness itself. This is a form of nature's fight response and when judiciously applied it is often the best choice.

Once unsatisfying consciousness is seen as the problem, increasing consciousness is almost always the best answer. In fact, raising consciousness just is the primary function of all existence. Evolution itself is the ongoing process of raising consciousness in the face of challenge.

Since consciousness is dynamic, transitional and relational, no single approach to raising consciousness will work in all situations. Most solutions, however, have a few things in common. They almost always begin with awareness of discomfort, and more often than not, the pain is associated with the illusions of self.

Self-centered problems tend to have an attention grabbing negative emotion attached. It just is the negative emotion which we experience as unsatisfying. Once aware of the negative emotion most of us look around for an external cause of our suffering. This is as far as most of us get in raising our consciousness. We fail to recognize that external events rarely cause unsatisfying consciousness. We squander the hours that could be otherwise worthwhile trying to change external factors which cannot possibly fix the real cause of our suffering. It is a form of insanity not unlike changing seats on the Titanic.

Sometimes while driving in my car, I find myself experiencing unsatisfying consciousness. It usually shows up in the form of anger. I become aware of my anger as I try to attach it to other drivers such as that idiot drifting into my lane. I have learned it is not the other driver that makes me angry. I know this is true because sometimes the very same behavior from others elicits a completely different response from me. Sometimes when someone drifts into my lane, I lovingly tap the horn as if to say "be careful my brother, go forth and sin no more." Other times I want to start a war. So it is not the behavior causing my anger.

The real problem is the anger itself. I remember feeling very angry at the people who first offered me this truth. They seemed to be having way too much fun telling me my anger was the real problem. I wanted them to agree with me that some external factor was causing my anger. They laughed and said, "No, the anger is the problem." At the time I didn't realize how important this new learning was for me in raising my own consciousness. I now see they were happy for me because they knew this was a big step in my development and they enjoyed seeing me grow.

The most likely explanation for the difference in my response to inattentive drivers drifting into my lane is that sometimes I have anger within me which only emerges into overt consciousness when someone shows up to give me a convenient place to put it. Only then do I awaken to my anger. "Aha, now I see it is you, the evil lane drifter who has made me angry."

When this happens there are only three options, do nothing, reduce consciousness or raise consciousness. Anger, it should be noted, is not a very good response to the challenge of safe driving. It is much better to be calm and aware.

Here is a little procedure for elevating consciousness. It is a way of bringing the boiling cauldron back down to a happy simmer. Let's say you are in the grocery store and you realize you are experiencing unsatisfying consciousness. As the negative emotion wells up inside of you and the anger emerges into your awareness, you look around for an external cause for your discomfort and you notice the shopper ahead of you in the ten item express line has eleven items. The effrontery!

It is here we remember, when faced with unsatisfying consciousness the universe offers only three options; immobility, retreat or advance. Being in line at a grocery store, you can quickly reduce your consciousness by grabbing a gossip magazine or candy bar. That is why they put them there.

Alternatively, you can choose to sit with your unsatisfactory consciousness in a state of tonic immobility and suffer the unrequited desire for a different state of consciousness. If neither of these options appeals to you, and I hope they do not, your only other option is to raise your consciousness. That's okay because raising consciousness just is the primary purpose of all existence.

If raising consciousness is the primary purpose, then everything else, including shopping, is at best a secondary goal. Here is some very good news. All secondary goals can be used to advance the primary purpose. Even bad news is good news because the disturbance you are experiencing has provided you with the motivation for growth. As the sage advised, "be grateful for the ripples on the pond."

Being aware of unsatisfying consciousness is the first step in the consciousness raising procedure. The next step is to ask yourself "what is the problem?" Most people will assume the problem is the eleven-item woman in the ten-item line. They will say something like, "I am angry because that woman has too many items and I am in a hurry." "She thinks she owns this place." "What is this world coming to?" But because you are reading this book you know the truth. The real problem is unsatisfying consciousness itself so you can move on to the next step of the consciousness raising process which is to ask yourself this simple question. "Who is disturbed?"

Simply by asking the question, you have already begun to elevate your consciousness because the "you" is no longer the disturbed one; rather, the "you" is the "presence" asking the question. You have shifted into being the observer of your consciousness rather than being the disturbed consciousness itself. In asking the question, you have created a space around the disturbance from which you can begin to extricate yourself should you choose to do so.

After asking "who is disturbed?" And thereby becoming the "presence" observing the disturbance, the next step in the process is to ask yourself this second critical question. "Wouldn't I like to know what this experience would be like without having any desire to change it?" "To experience the experience as it is with full acceptance?" When we become open to this idea, the suffering subsides because we are no longer identifying as the sufferer; instead, we are the witness to the natural unfolding transitions of consciousness.

Like all new learning, raising consciousness involves the formation of new association networks within the brain. As new clusters of neurons are recruited to form the new association network out of which new elevated consciousness will emerge, they begin to develop a cohesive identity as the "presence" observing our consciousness rather than the self-centered language-based ego doing the suffering.

Surrendering to reality is a skill, and like all new learning, it improves with practice. As we practice identifying as the presence observing consciousness, the new association networks responsible for inducing our new awareness becomes a working part of the mind. From this new and growing perspective, we don't take our experiences so personally because we know we are much more than the illusion of a separate language based ego mind.

This does not mean we accept life's circumstances without taking corrective actions. The exercise is simply a way of directly addressing the challenge of unsatisfying consciousness. Take corrective actions if they are warranted, but try to do so with greater consciousness. Remember there are only three options for dealing with your unsatisfying consciousness. Choose wisely.

Gazzaniga, Michael (1967). "The Split Brain in Man." Scientific American. 217 (2): 24–29.

Keenan J.P., Nelson A., O'Connor, M. & Pascual-Leone, A. Neurology: Self-recognition and the right hemisphere Nature 409, 305 (18 January 2001) | 67

Bolte Taylor, Jill (2008). My Stroke of Insight: A Brain Scientist's Personal Journey. Viking. ISBN 978-0-670-02074-4

12 AWAKENING

We understand the cosmos through disassembly and analysis of the elements and systems from which it is made. Elements come together to form systems and systems come together to form the universe. Understanding emerges as we compare and contrast the shifting properties of the elements and systems under consideration.

Elements and systems interact in a dynamic transitional and relational way. The properties of a system differ from the properties of its elements in the same way a book differs from a collection of words. When a collection of words becomes dynamically, transitionally, and relationally associated with each other, it becomes a book and understanding emerges from the analysis of its elements.

Since understanding emerges through disassembly and analysis, it makes sense as elements come together to form new systems, the new systems exhibit new emergent properties. Life, the universe, and everything manifests from an infinite array of continually interacting elements and systems combining, disassembling, and recombining again to form ever new systems with ever new emergent properties.

Subatomic particles come together to form atoms, which come together to form molecules, which come together to form compounds, which come together to form amino acids, which come together to form proteins which combine with carbohydrates and lipids to form cells, which come together to form tissues, which come together to form organs, which come together to form organ systems, which come together to form organisms, which come together to form communities, which come together to form ecosystems, and so it goes. Each new layer of complexity depends upon and emerges from the properties of its constituent elements, and with each new layer, we see new emergent properties. The properties of everything hinge upon the properties of everything else; it is all thoroughly interconnected; the universe is one.

The signals inducing consciousness also interact in this reductionist and emergent way. Like everything else in the universe, consciousness is dynamic, transitional and relational because, like everything else, it emerges from the dynamic, transitional and relational signal transfer patterns between antecedent expressions of dynamic, transitional and relational signal transfer. The constant flux between the elements and systems which induce consciousness make understanding a challenge.

Isaac Newton had a similar problem when he studied gravity. To better understand the dynamic behaviors of objects under the influence of gravity he invented a new math called calculus. With his new math, Newton noted the relationship between mass, change in position and change in time of balls rolling down inclined planes and so derived the universal law of gravitation. He then realized his formula for gravity described both the motion of balls on inclined planes and the movement of planets across the heavens.

It was an important advance in human understanding. What seemed magical before was now recognized as the orderly expression of natural law. Though the discovery allows for prediction of the rate of change of falling bodies within a gravity field leading directly to placing a man on the moon, it did not explain how or why gravity does its work. Instead, it described the rules by which gravity's unknown cause operates.

When we see the same dynamic, transitional and

relational signal transfer process inducing consciousness in everything from microorganisms on up to the human brain, here too we should recognize we are witnessing a fundamental force of nature. And when we extend our analysis to include inorganic matter and see the same fingerprint of dynamic, transitional and relational signal transfer at work, we can begin to feel we're on to something big.

Since dynamic, transitional and relational signal transfer induces consciousness in everything from microbes on up to the human brain, it is reasonable to suspect that dynamic, transitional and relational signal transfer produces consciousness wherever it occurs. Just as all mass induces gravity, it is reasonable to believe all patterns of dynamic, transitional and relational signal transfer induce consciousness.

Furthermore, because everything in the universe interacts through dynamic, transitional and relational signal transfer, we see a constant conjunction between dynamic, transitional and relational signal transfer and both mind and matter. The entire universe is an infinitely complex dynamic, transitional and relational signal transfer machine inducing both mind and matter expressed as a never-ending cascading array of "associated separateness," or if you prefer "dissociated oneness." The universe is one.

From this perspective, the best answer to the question "what is consciousness?" may be the counter question "is there anything other than consciousness?" At the deepest and most fundamental level of analysis, both mind and matter emerge from the same dynamic, transitional and relational signal transfer process. The signal transfer patterns which induce consciousness and the signal transfer patterns which induce matter are one and the same. The associations of dynamic, transitional and relational signal transfer induce everything.

Even gravity emerges from a signal transfer induced process. The association between mass and space/time is just another expression of consciousness. Gravity is the curvature of space in response to mass. This means even empty space has awareness. Space must be aware of mass and mass must be aware of space for there to be an association. In the absence of some sort of signal based interaction between mass and space, there could be no association and therefore no gravity. Everything is signal based awareness; the universe is one.

As radical as this may sound, it is not a new idea. Eastern philosophies, Hindu Idealism, and many American Indian cultures describe the universe in terms consistent with a single interconnected unity of consciousness. In the West, the Hegelian idea of "the Absolute" and Carl Jung's collective unconscious are also declarations of universal oneness. And now from the world of physics, we hear voices suggesting consciousness is a state of matter. When all of these schools of thought converge with our observations of the natural world, we gain confidence that dynamic, transitional and relational signal transfer, whether between the particles that make up physical matter or between the neurons making up gray matter, form the association matrix out of which the very fabric of the universe emerges. Signals of association are the fundamental components of reality through which all similarities and differences get expressed. "Compare and contrast, that's all there is!"

The entire universe is a buzzing cacophony of continually interacting dynamic, transitional and relational signal transfer between an ever-changing array of elements and systems inducing a kaleidoscope of emergent mind and matter. Everything which exists; every subatomic particle, every atom, every molecule and every compound participates in this never ending dance of dynamic, transitional and relational signal transfer which is the hallmark of all mind and matter.

The simple hydrogen atom, by its mere existence, exhibits what could be called "hydrogen consciousness." The contrast between the signals indicating the boundary between hydrogen and non-hydrogen allow for the detection of hydrogen by other systems whenever hydrogen is sensed, but at a deeper level, the properties of hydrogen consciousness emerge from the pattern of dynamic, transitional and relational signal transfer between the proton and the electron making up the hydrogen atom itself.

Hydrogen is the simplest element on the chemist's periodic table. Each hydrogen atom contains one positively charged proton and one negatively charged electron. These two subatomic particles are dynamically joined together by the electromagnetic force causing particles with opposite charge to attract.

For hydrogen to maintain its "hydrogen-ness" the proton must have some signal based "awareness" of the electron and electron must have some signal based "awareness" of the proton. Without these signals and their detections, there could be no association. The signals and detections between protons and electrons are the awareness of information transfer. The properties of "hydrogen consciousness" emerge from the signal transfer pattern facilitating the association between hydrogen proton and electron.

Each element of the periodic table has a different number and configuration of protons, neutrons, and electrons. As such, each exhibits a different pattern of signal transfer between its constituent protons, neutrons, and electrons. Because everything interacts through signal transfer, the unique signal transfer pattern of each element causes it to interact uniquely. It is the pattern of signal transfer between protons, neutrons, and electrons which gives each elements its unique set of properties making each element distinct.

Hydrogen atoms at standard room temperature and pressure tend to pair up with other hydrogen atoms to form molecules of hydrogen gas (H2). They join together with a covalent bond made through dynamically sharing their electrons. The dynamic, transitional and relational signal transfer pattern between bonded pairs of hydrogen atoms gives hydrogen gas its distinctive set of properties, which is to say, determines the way hydrogen interacts with the rest of the universe. One property of hydrogen gas is flammability (think Hindenburg).

The name hydrogen comes from the words hydro (water) and Gen (to make) because when it burns, the byproduct is water. To burn hydrogen just is to combine hydrogen molecules (H2) with oxygen molecules (O2). This dynamic, transitional and relational process releases energy in the form of heat and light as the hydrogen and oxygen molecules disassemble and rearrange to form new molecules of what might be called "water consciousness." This new arrangement of the very same atoms has a new set of emergent properties induced by the new pattern of signal transfer between the three atoms now joined to make molecules of water (H2O). An emergent property of water is the ability to extinguish fires.

Another property of water is the capacity to be separated back into hydrogen and oxygen. This separation can occur through electrolysis. Apply a direct electrical current to electrodes immersed in water and the hydrogen atoms of the water molecules will be attracted to the negatively charged cathode while the oxygen atoms are attracted to the positively charged anode. This causes the water to separate back into hydrogen and oxygen seen as tiny gas bubbles forming at their respective electrodes. The amount of energy required to separate water into hydrogen and oxygen is the same as the amount of energy liberated when hydrogen and oxygen burn. This equivalence is the conservation of energy law stating that energy can neither be created nor destroyed, only transformed.

Now, most would agree a glass of water has very little personality. Not much consciousness going on here. The signal transfer patterns of association between water molecules at standard temperature and pressure are dynamic and relational, but they are not very transitional. The same goes for a container of hydrogen and oxygen gas.

During transformation, however, we see a shifting of emergent properties along with a shifting of signal transfer patterns which is similar to the dynamic, transitional, and relational signal transfer of simple consciousness such as the patellar reflex.

The shifting signal patterns inducing the shifting properties of burning hydrogen are consistent with the shifting patterns of signals inducing reflex behaviors. In both cases a dynamic, transitional and relational signal transfer process results in behavior.

Some will recoil at the idea that dynamic, transitional and relational signal transfer patterns express consciousness. Their resistance probably stems from false assumptions about the nature of their own "self.-concept." When consciousness believes itself to be separate and apart from the rest of the universe, misunderstandings emerge.

Consciousness, broadly defined, is simply the way stuff interacts. Just because the signal transfer patterns of inanimate objects sometimes appear to be self-limiting as seen from the narrow time frame of common human experience does not mean these signal transfer patterns are devoid of consciousness.

Dynamic, transitional and relational signal transfer induces all consciousness. The very fabric of the universe emerges from these interactive transitional signal transfer events. Remember, consciousness can not be measured directly, it can only be inferred through behavior. Everything which interacts (behaves) does so through dynamic, transitional and relational signal transfer consistent with the signal transfer patterns known to induce consciousness in other systems.

It is dynamic, transitional and relational signal transfer which induces all behavior and all consciousness. The behavior of both burning hydrogen and jerking quadriceps is the evidence of consciousness being induced by the dynamic, transitional and relational signal transfer events between the elements of systems experiencing the change.

At the next level down protons, neutrons, and electrons express what could be called proton, neutron and electron consciousness. Each of these subatomic particles has properties induced by the pattern of signal transfer between their interacting constituent elements.

The building blocks of protons, neutrons, and electrons are called quarks. There are six types of quarks; up, down, strange, charmed, top and bottom. Like everything else in the universe, quarks associate through dynamic, transitional and relational signal transfer.

"Proton consciousness," for example, emerges from the signal transfer pattern of association between two up quarks and one down quark. It is the signal transfer pattern between associated quarks which induce the emergent properties of protons, neutrons, and electrons in the same way the signals transfer patterns between protons, neutrons and electrons induce the properties of atoms.

This logic extends to string theory which posits quarks to be one-dimensional vibrating energy packets called strings. Each type of string vibrates in a particular way thereby distinguishing it from all the other kinds of strings making up the particle zoo now thought to be the ultimate building blocks of reality. The ideas of signal transfer induced mind and matter continue to apply.

The vibration of a string is an oscillation between two or more energy states. Each transitional position in the oscillation cycle has a particular property in contrast to all other states. The signals indicating the shifting states of string consciousness induce the string's properties and determine the way the string interacts with the rest of the universe. It is the fluctuation of signals between oscillating states which is the expression out of which string consciousness emerges.

It is reasonable to assume, in time, we will discover some new even more fundamental building block of reality underlying the structure of strings. For argument's sake let's call these as yet undiscovered elements "threads." The discovery of threads will hinge upon the discovery of a signal pattern distinguishing threads from non-threads. When this occurs, it will be the signal patterns of threads which dictate the way threads associate with the rest of universe thereby inducing "thread consciousness."

The signal patterns indicating the existence of threads will be as fundamental to thread existence as any other property we may assign. Because of the constant conjunction between thread signal patterns and thread existence, it will make sense to say thread signal patterns induce thread properties which are an expression of "thread consciousness." These signal patterns will not only induce the properties of threads; they will constitute the only essential component of thread existence. Without these signals and their detections, there would be no evidence for thread existence at all.

It may be tempting to conclude emergent consciousness is an attribute of all matter, but signal patterns inducing consciousness also emerge from non-material wave and charge phenomena as well. The same principles apply. It is the dynamically associated signal transfer patterns indicating the presence of wave or difference in charge which induce the subsequent wave or charge "consciousness."

The rule seems to be, anything detectable, in other words, anything which interacts through dynamic, transitional and relational signal transfer, expresses consciousness. Signals of information transfer are the fundamental building blocks of reality. Consciousness, the universe, and everything emerges from dynamic, transitional and relational signal transfer. The universe is one.

The more elemental forms of consciousness which emerge from the associations between subatomic particles are nowhere near the complexity of the "I think therefore I am" level of consciousness sometimes seen in the human brain. Self-awareness requires many compounded layers of dynamic, transitional and relational signal transfer to emerge.

Expecting self-awareness from subatomic particle consciousness would be like expecting the spontaneous emergence of the Mona Lisa directly from pigments and canvas. Clearly, many intermediate steps are necessary for the emergence of a masterpiece.

Though human consciousness emerges most directly from the dynamic, transitional and relational signal transfer patterns between neurons in the brain many steps removed from the signal transfer patterns of strings, the same process of dynamic, transitional and relational signal transfer occurs throughout. We see this echoed in the mathematically inspired work of graphic artist MC Escher with his representations of worlds within worlds. It is easy to see why this work has such broad appeal; it resonates with our deeper neurological association networks.

Lest we be lulled into believing we have a complete understanding of the universe, there are reasons to believe complete understanding will always elude us. Gödel's incompleteness theorems are two proven formulations of mathematical logic which establish the limits of all but the most trivial systems capable of performing an arithmetic. An arithmetic is the dynamic, transitional, relational system of association between the abstractions we call numbers. It is likely all dynamic, transitional and relational systems are computational in nature.

Gödel's theorems are important for understanding the limits of computational systems. The first incompleteness theorem states no consistent system of axioms whose theorems can be listed by an "effective procedure" is capable of proving all truths about the relations between the natural numbers. For any such system, there will always be statements about the natural numbers which are true, but unprovable from within the system itself.

The second incompleteness theorem extends the first by showing that no system can fully demonstrate its own internal consistency. This work suggests computational systems are unexplainable from within the system itself. The idea makes sense because dynamic, transitional and relational systems are by definition relational and therefore dependent upon other systems for their validity. The universe simply may not allow for a complete understanding of the universe from within the universe itself.

The closer we get to the edges of understanding of any system, the more logic itself seems to break down. At the extremes of scale, for instance, both the very small and the very large have problems. Our compare and contrast engine of understanding simply cannot rationally categorize all the data into one fully integrated system. The system as a whole just doesn't seem to make sense.

At the subatomic level, for example, matter and light have both wave and particle properties. In some contexts, they behave like particles while in others they behave like waves. From a rational perspective, particles must either exist or not exist. Common sense tells us an object can not "be" and "not be." In the face of this seemingly incontrovertible truth, the universe refuses to conform to our common sense notions of existence. Our observations defy logic.

At the other end of the spectrum, on the cosmological scale, we see theories describing an infinite, unbounded universe which also seems to defy logic. Some imagine an infinite universe as part of a meta-universe or multiverse containing an infinite number of ever expanding parallel universes. Each of these infinite universes extends boundlessly in all directions making up an infinity of infinite universes. It boggles the mind. With theories like these, any comfort we take in believing we have a firm grasp on reality may be a bit optimistic. In some ways, the universe simply does not add up.

Still, we shouldn't be too discouraged by the limits of our understanding. There was a time, not very long ago when people thought the Earth was flat. It was believed a giant turtle carried the flat Earth on its back. There is the story of an astronomer giving a lecture about the Earth, the solar system, and the Milky Way galaxy. After the lecture, a little old lady stood up and scolded the scientist by saying, "Rubbish, the world is a flat plate on the back of a giant tortoise." When the scientist replied, "What is the tortoise standing on?" The little old lady said, "You're very clever, young man, but its turtles all the way down!" We enjoy this story in part because it resonates with truth about the limits of understanding. From a certain perspective, at the edges of knowledge, the little old lady was right. It might as well be turtles all the way down.

So, it appears there are some things we just don't get to know. Then there are other things we do know which seem to be positively magical. For instance, physics tells us that matter and energy are equivalent. To calculate the amount of energy (E) in a given amount of matter, simply multiply the mass (m) by the speed of light (c) squared ($E=mc^2$). This all means a small amount of matter equals a lot of energy. The power of the atomic bomb comes from the transformation of matter directly into energy. So, matter is energy, and energy is matter; presto chango, just like magic.

Other things, which at first appear to be magical, are later found to be easily understandable ordered events. Mitosis is a type of cell division which results in the formation of two daughter cells with the same chromosomal DNA as the parent cell. People used to think this process was guided by some sort of magical "élan vital" or vital cosmic life force forever beyond human understanding.

Seeing mitosis through a microscope is like witnessing a beautifully choreographed ballet of chromosomes as they replicate and dance to opposite sides of the cell just before cell division. Though the chemistry of the process was well understood, no one could explain the mechanism of action until the discovery of the structure of DNA. Once the double helix coding system of DNA was known, it all made perfect sense and the need for supernatural explanations vanished (poof).

The metamorphosis of a caterpillar into a butterfly is another example of a seemingly magical process. Most imagine a butterfly's transformation within the chrysalis to be simply the growing of wings and legs, but a much more dramatic process takes place. The caterpillar essentially liquefies to become completely transformed. Surprisingly, even after this dramatic transformation, butterflies can retain "memories" learned as caterpillars.

Blackison, Casey, and Weiss (2008) of Georgetown University classically conditioned caterpillars to avoid a usually neutral chemical by pairing the chemical with a mild electric shock. Caterpillars so conditioned retained their aversion to the formally neutral chemical even after becoming butterflies. Research like this is compelling because it seems to suggest a transcendent caterpillar soul.

The word soul is almost synonymous with the word consciousness; however, the word soul implies immortality in a way the word consciousness does not. When a butterfly retains learning from a previous incarnation as a caterpillar, we see an aspect of consciousness seemingly able to transcend the corporeal body.

Because we understand the nature of classically conditioned associations and the physical structures involved, we now know this example of retained learning does not really support the idea of an immortal soul. It does, however, raise the question.

When considering evidence for the existence of an immortal soul, it is best to tread lightly because here we find the deeply held beliefs of people who are sometimes easily offended. Before beginning in earnest, we should reaffirm our allegiance to truth. Nothing would please me more than to write a book which offended no one. I have done my best to achieve this goal. However, there is simply no way to fully explore the nature of consciousness without also coming to terms with this important question.

Let me be clear. The answer to the question "do humans possess an immortal soul?" is, we do not know. Though there is no scientifically valid evidence to support the existence of an immortal soul, no one can say with assurance the soul does not exist because it is logically impossible to prove the nonexistence of anything. No one can say with certainty Santa Claus does not exist. In both cases, there will always be a thin thread of hope for believers based largely on the argument that the absence of evidence is not evidence of absence. Though true, it is incumbent upon the believer to provide rational support for their beliefs.

Some may argue that the belief in an immortal soul is a harmless or even beneficial position to take. They seem to think that this belief encourages good behavior. It is true there are many shining examples of good behavior from people who believe in the existence of an immortal soul. It is also true there are many examples of appalling behavior from sincere believers. There is no evidence for any net gain in prosperity. Sadly, there seems to be no limit to the amount of pain and suffering some believers will inflict on others in their sincere efforts to save immortal souls.

Today we see the belief in an immortal soul somehow separate and apart from the rest of the universe as a prime motivator of violence and mayhem across the globe. We know human consciousness is layered and complex. Deep down, many "earnest believers" doubt their own convictions. This causes psychological dissonance and distress as they grapple with a consciousness unable to reconcile the contradictions brought on by the absence of empirical support for their own beliefs. This psychological distress is all too often expressed through anger and violence.

The evidence strongly suggests human consciousness, like all consciousness, is an emergent property of dynamic, transitional and relational signal transfer between the elements of nature. There is a constant conjunction between the dynamic, transitional and relational signal transfer patterns between neurons and human consciousness. Also, whenever these dynamic, transitional and relational signal transfer patterns cease, all evidence for consciousness also ceases.

Additionally, when structures known to be responsible for specific aspects of consciousness are damaged, we reliably see deficits in the respective domains of cognitive function. There are many cases affecting almost every aspect of human consciousness which provide support for this idea. Face blindness results from damage to the right fusiform gyrus which is responsible for coordinating the systems of facial perception and memory. Similarly, damage to Broca's area reliably results in speech deficits. These findings and many others like them all strongly suggest human consciousness just is an emergent property of dynamic, transitional and relational signal transfer between neurons.

Furthermore, because consciousness is always relational, it logically follows that all "individual" consciousness is an extension of one single vast interconnected cascading signal transfer process. Consciousness is always dynamic, transitional and relational and therefore always interconnected. An immortal soul somehow separate and apart from the rest of the universe is, from a signal processing perspective, a logical impossibility. The universe is a fully integrated system of signal transfer. The universe is one.

Most people experience consciousness as the narrative emerging from their language based neurological association networks. These abstractions and reflections of reality originally evolved to induce a consciousness able to deal with the demands of a complex social world. These neurological networks then fabricated the abstraction of abstractions we call the self-concept.

Self-concept is the illusion of a dissociated consciousness separate and apart from the rest of reality. This illusion is useful because it facilitates the compare and contrast evaluations of self versus others allowing for more efficient interactions in a complex social world. However, being useful and being ontologically real are not the same thing. The self-concept is an abstraction of abstractions at least twice removed from reality! The self-concept is not real.

We can appreciate the way the abstractions of a self-concept play out by considering the hidden toy scenario. This scenario is the thought experiment wherein two children are playing together in a room. The first child places a toy train in the toy chest and tells the second child "do not touch my train" as he exits the room. The second child then moves the train from the toy chest to the closet. The question becomes; where will the first child look for the train when he returns?

Children younger than four or five usually expect him to look in the closet because young children lack the perspective of other minds as being different from their own. They have yet to fully develop the abstraction of abstractions we call the self-concept which enables us to compare and contrast our own awareness with the likely awareness of others. In the absence of a fully developed self-concept, young children lack a functional awareness of the likely awareness of others.

Though the self-concept is useful, it is not who we are. Instead, it is a psychological framework of neurological associations out of which emerges the illusion of a separate self. It is a natural phase of mental development. Self-concept is useful, but when it believes itself to be ontologically real, separate and apart from the rest of the universe, problems do occur. Rigid identification as a self-concept can overwhelm a mind the same way cancer overwhelms a body.

In years to come, as humanity develops greater consciousness, believing the self-concept to be a separate immortal soul apart from the rest of the universe will be seen as a normal stage of incomplete human development, not unlike a child's inability to conceptualize the awareness of other minds. As consciousness increases, there will be a natural shift from a rigid identification as a self-concept to the more accurate global identification as universal consciousness. Clinicians will diagnose those who cling to the idea of being a separate immortal soul somehow apart from the rest of the universe in the same light as those who believe themselves to be Napoleon.

Human consciousness is much more than the illusion of a separate self-concept. All consciousness is integrated with all other consciousness. There is but one vast cascading dynamic, transitional and relational signal transfer process which is the universe itself. We are the universe. The universe is one. A full awaking to this truth offers a free and easy sense of infinite possibility sometimes described as being like the ocean entering the drop.

Everything that is detectable, which is to say everything, exhibits the signal transfer patterns of consciousness. The time scale of everyday human experience usually obscures the true nature of our fully interactive universe. Even the seemingly unchanging crystal structure of a diamond expresses dynamic, transitional and relational consciousness as evidenced by the behavior of change.

In spite of the popular advertising campaign to the contrary, diamonds are not forever. Given enough time, at standard room temperature and pressure, the crystal structure of carbon atoms making up a diamond will spontaneously degrade into the lower level energy graphite state.

And, when the graphite state carbon atoms are placed under enough pressure and temperature, they will transform back into diamond. Life, the universe, and everything is continually undergoing dynamic, transitional and relational signal transfer induced transformation which is the telltale sign of consciousness.

Consciousness, the universe, and everything emerges from the interactive dynamic, transitional and relational signal transfer patterns between the elements of systems. When we recognize that both mind and matter emerge from the same dynamic, transitional and relational signal transfer process, we benifit because this wider perspective provides support for the unification of mind and matter. We have found a single process which describes both mental and physical reality. We have discovered a new universal law of nature.

Recognizing that signal transfer patterns induce both mind and matter or that mind and matter are the expressions of signal transfer may at first seem to do little for advancing our understanding. Some might even say, "It may as well be turtles all the way down." However, by recognizing signal transfer to be the basis of all mind and all matter we can safely and assuredly jettison ideas of separation in favor of a more accurate perspective of a universe of mind and matter structured as a single indivisible whole. The universe really is one.

The author Joseph Campbell shared a story illuminating the oneness of universe. It takes place on a bridge in Australia where, sadly, young people all too often go to commit suicide by jumping to their deaths. A young man had already stepped over the guardrail as the police car approached. When the officer closest to the young man saw him beginning to jump, he lunged forward to save him. Their combined momentum now caused both men to begin to fall. Just then, and with no margin for error, the second officer grabbed the first pulling the two men back from certain death.

Later, as a reporter interviewed the first officer, the question was asked: "why did you do it?" From a rational perspective, it made no sense. The officer had a wife and children who were dependent upon him. He didn't even know the young man, and yet he risked everything for a total stranger.

The officer's response was probably more honest than he himself knew. He said, "I had to." When the young man tried to jump, the illusion of separateness dropped out and the reality of oneness broke through. He did have to risk everything to save that young man, because in that brief moment, for all practical purposes, he was the young man.

Altruistic behaviors naturally emerge with the recognition of need and the dissolving of ego boundaries. Whenever we hear these stories, we are comforted because they remind us of our universal oneness. When asked about their helping behaviors, the helpers themselves are often taken aback. They have trouble understanding just what all the fuss is about. To them, their altruistic behavior seems entirely justified. They assume anyone would do the same in a similar circumstance. Their behavior naturally flowed from the recognition of need and the realization of oneness. It is as if the motivation for altruism originated outside of the self.

This brings us to another important question closely related to the question of an immortal soul. I am referring here to the issue of free will. Philosophers have wrestled with the idea free will since time out of memory. It is perhaps the central question in the long debate.

Most people believe in both free will and cause and effect, but this is a logical contradiction. Free will and cause and effect cannot both be true. Once again, in answering this important question, I want to be entirely clear. The answer to the question, "Do humans possess a free will?" is, we do not know.

We may have no choice in the way we come to identify ourselves. Identifying as an immortal soul somehow separate and apart from the rest of reality, or identifying as a facet of universal consciousness may in the last analysis be a function of strict determinism.

Though the universe is a fully integrated system of cascading dynamic, transitional and relational signal transfer operating in strict accordance with the immutable laws of physics and chemistry, we should remain open to the possibility that a group of bipedal ape descendants on a tiny blue-green planet orbiting a yellow star at a distance of about 93 million miles is the one exception to the rule.

Or as Voltaire put it: ".... that all nature and all the stars should obey eternal laws, and that there should be one little animal five feet tall which, despite these laws, could always act as suited its own caprice."

It is doubtful we'll ever have a definitive answer to the age-old question of free will because a test for free will appears to be a logical impossibility. Any analysis must assume the capacity for free will on the part of the test taker for the test taker to meaningfully respond to the test items. In spite of this assumption, it will always be possible for a test taker to respond in such a way to indicate the presence of free will, but to do so in a deterministic manner thereby invalidating the process.

There is, however, some research which seems to shed a little light on the nature of human consciousness and free will. In 1983, a study by Benjamin Libet examined the timing of the brain's signal to move a finger and the timing of the subject's decision to move their own finger. By measuring the activity of neurons in the primary motor cortex responsible for initiating all voluntary muscle movement and the timing of the subject's awareness of their decision to move their finger, researchers discovered that subjects reported knowledge of their decision to move their own finger only after the neurological sequence for moving the finger had already begun. In other words, the brain commits to moving the finger even before the subject is aware of their own decision to move their own finger. This surprising result is consistent with a consciousness operating under the illusion of self-determination arising only after a retrospective evaluation of behavior.

This all aligns nicely with what we have learned about the cascading order of effects of consciousness. It makes sense that our decision to initiate action arises from a level in the order of effects of consciousness operating below language based processing. Language based processing is, after all, the abstraction of perceptions designed to simulate reality.

The Libet study suggests that our language processing is more of a play-by-play retrospective color commentator on experience rather than the quarterback directing the team down the field to victory. We are not our language-based thoughts. We are not our self-concept.

These findings naturally beg the question, if we are not the story we tell ourselves about ourselves, then who or what is running the show? Since choice, if it exists, emerges from the association networks operating below the level of language based processing, how far back in the cascading sequence in the order of effects of consciousness do we go to find the origins of the will? Since the order of effects of consciousness extend all the way back to the signal transfer patterns of the universe itself, we must acknowledge the possibility of a will external to the human body. It may be the human will is not localized at all. The will to move a finger and the will to spin a galaxy may, in fact, be one and the same.

Even in the absence of free will, the illusion of free will is a useful feature of language based processing. Language, like everything else, evolved to advance survival. The ego must see itself as independent from others to calculate individual versus other survival probabilities. We know this illusion promotes survival, or else nature would not select it, but that does not necessarily mean there is a free will able to choose between behaviors. It is possible for the illusion of free will to emerge from the mandates of biology and experience. We simply can not know whether it is the universe or the individual ultimately responsible for choice.

Freewill suggests a consciousness separate and apart from the rest of reality. Our language based simulations conjure a narrative of self-concept which coalesces into a sense of separateness we call the self-concept. This consciousness then awakens to its own mortality as it calculates the absolute certainty of its own death. This inescapable threat to existence generates a persistent sense of anxiety of impending doom. Since death is certain, the only possibility for a return to a sense of safety and security is the fabrication of an immortal soul with a free will.

Though these fears and fabrications are easy to understand, they are not at all based in reality. The idea of a separate self apart from the rest of the universe is an illusion emerging from the abstractions of abstractions we call the self-concept manufactured by the language based processing centers of the brain. When thinking of self-concept and mortality, we would do well to remember who we think we are, and what we are afraid of losing, in a very real way, does not even exist. To be afraid of death is to be afraid of nothing at all.

Self-concept is a valuable tool for getting along in the world. There are many threats which require the perspective of an independent agent in opposition to others to be effectively countered. Rigid adherence to this perspective, however, must either include the anxiety that comes with the knowledge of certain death, or the delusion of an immortal soul separate and apart from the rest of the universe. Our findings on the nature of consciousness, the universe and everything now offer a new option.

Like the wave-particle duality of light, human consciousness is an expression of a context driven duality between self-concept and universal mind. To see things accurately in their truest perspective we must develop a flexibility in our consciousness. We must learn to shift between identification as self-concept and identification as universal consciousness. Both perspectives are true from within their context, and both are necessary for healthy mental adjustment.

A healthy consciousness resists the urge to become too rigidly identified as either a language based narrative of self-concept or the integrated awareness of universal mind. Rigid adherence to either perspective is incomplete. Instead, we must be open to shifting between these modes of identification in adaptive ways as the situation requires.

But, you may ask, who or what is shifting between self-concept and universal mind? The best answer to this question may be the universe itself awakening to the nature of consciousness, the universe and everything.

Libet B, Gleason CA, Wright EW, Pearl DK. (1983) Brain Sep; 106 (Pt 3):623-42. Time of conscious intention to act in relation to onset of cerebral activity (readiness-potential). The unconscious initiation of a freely voluntary act.

Blackiston DJ, Silva Casey E, Weiss MR (2008) PLoS ONE 3(3): e1736. doi:10.1371/journal.pone.0001736 Retention of Memory through Metamorphosis: Can a Moth Remember What It Learned As a Caterpillar?

ABOUT THE AUTHOR

Alex Milov is a Licensed Psychotherapist. He received his undergraduate and graduate psychology degrees from Florida International University where he studied General Psychology, Industrial Organizational Psychology and Counseling Psychology. He went on to become Board Certified in Rapid Trauma Resolution and taught psychology at the ATI College of Health. He currently sees individuals, couples and groups in private practice in Saint Petersburg Florida.